Master Builders of Modern Psychology

Master Builders
of
Modern Psychology

From Freud to Skinner

J.D. Keehn

New York University Press
Washington Square, New York

First published in the U.S.A. in 1996 by
NEW YORK UNIVERSITY PRESS
Washington Square
New York, N.Y. 10003

Library of Congress Cataloging-in-Publication Data

Keehn, J.D.
   Master builders of modern psychology : from Freud to Skinner /
J.D. Keehn.
     p. cm.
   Includes bibliographical references and index.
   ISBN 0-8147-4685-3
   1. Psychology—History—20th century. 2. Psychology–
–History—19th century. 3. Behaviorism (Psychology)—History.
I. Title.
BF105.K44   1996
150'.9—dc20   95-51968
                                                  CIP

Printed in Great Britain

Foreword

J.D. 'Peter' Keehn, who died shortly after completing this book, was a psychologist who often mused on the diverse nature of his profession. He himself was a man of many parts. His initial training was in mathematics and physics at University College, London, and after graduate studies at Stanford and the Maudsley Hospital he spent ten years at the American University in Beirut before crossing the Atlantic to work first in the United States and then in Canada. His profession took him from university teaching to guidance clinics, to the Ontario Addiction Research Foundation and latterly to his students and his laboratory at York University. His writings ranged from the Rorschach to research ethics, from alcoholism to education and mental testing. Although he built a reputation as a radical, experimental behaviourist he could understand, though perhaps not wholly agree with, Maslow, a leading humanistic psychologist, when he said, 'I am Freudian and I am behaviouristic and I am humanistic.'

Freud and Skinner both rejected psychology's eclectic acceptance of the variety of approaches taught in its schools, and their passionate promotion of what they considered to be the 'truth' sometimes brought them bitter criticism. Keehn, in a long and productive academic career, returned to a consideration of these men and this book reflects his own fascination with both mentalistic and mechanistic views of the human condition. The affection and admiration of the author's colleagues for his intellectual agility and his personal charm will be reinforced and their consciousness raised by this, his last work.

Michael Cowles
Professor of Psychology
York University, Canada

Contents

To Nancy Luxmore Keehn

Preface

I have been studying how I may compare
This prison where I live unto the world
And for because the world is populous,
And here is not a creature but myself,
I cannot do it; ...
       Shakespeare, *Richard II*, Act V, Scene v

Somebody once quipped that whereas successive generations of physical scientists stood on each other's shoulders, successive generations of social scientists stepped on each other's faces. The remark may not be profound, but it digs a foundation for the construction of this book. In it, I intend to show that some of the stepped-on faces are the shoulders on which modern psychology was built.

'Who am I, Rupert?' a Timothy Findley fictional character asks her psychiatrist. 'Doesn't it depend on who is looking? And when?' he answers.[1] This answer is the guide for the reading of this book, which may be taken as an unusual history of systems of psychology (unusual in that it contains little history and shows how the rival systems complement as much as compete with one another), a guide to the study of personality and the practice of psychotherapy, or a refocusing of behavioural science from prediction to chaos.

Whichever of these it is, depends on who is looking and when. Few readers are likely to be attracted to all parts of the book at once, but my hope is that most will find different parts instructive from time to time. Nevertheless the psychiatrist's answer is not the one the questioner wanted and it is not an answer a reader expects either. At least there has to be a characterization of the person or a title for the book.

Just as an egocentric characterization inadequately describes a person, so a single title inadequately describes a book. One title is not enough. This book might have been called *In Remembrance of Things to Come*, for it can be read as a brief history of the future of psychology. This century has witnessed a paradigm shift in psychology as great as that in astronomy occasioned by Copernicus four centuries ago. Then, the shift was from a geocentric to a heliocentric view of the universe; now, the shift is from an intrapsychic to a transactional view of human experience and behaviour.[2] This shift is no easier to make than that begun by Copernicus, in fact probably harder because the illusion of egocentricity is more compelling than the illusion of geocentricity. The reasons for the psychological shift, and the steps that led up to it, are the conventional substance of this book.

I actually call the book *Master Builders of Modern Psychology*, leaving me free to elucidate particular systems, and the reader free to take my major thesis or leave it. In that case, the book is a history of scientific psychology's brief past through the ideas of individuals who contributed prominently to it. The subtitle *From Freud to Skinner* places the scope of the book between these twin peaks of modern psychology; to those who dislike the idea of peaks, *Freud and the Rivals* would serve equally well. Better still would be the elimination of systematists altogether, but that would necessitate an unacceptable rewriting of the history of psychology.[3] Unacceptable because psychology has two histories, a history of systems and a history of applications. The history of systems is like the history of science, and can discard the systematists (except in history books) as the prevailing scientific paradigm advances; the history of applications is like the history of the novel, for no matter how paradigms of literature evolve, the works of significant novelists are not discarded but preserved. Freud is such a significant novelist, although his psychoanalytic theories are inadequate as a systematic natural science of behaviour capable of underpinning an applied psychological science. In the end, psychology more than any other discipline has had the responsibility of uniting the subjective with the objective; now its responsibility is to unite action and transaction.

After some preliminaries concerning mind, behaviour and psychotherapy, setting the paradigmatic natures of psychology in place, the book begins with an account of Freudian dynamics from first principles, and describes how Freud developed situational (S), organismic (O), and behavioural (R) variables in the explanation of comportment. This is followed by rival accounts of the O-variable by Jung, Eysenck, and Boss, and of the S-variable by Adler and Sullivan. On the way, a sketch of the R-variable shifts the focus from intrapsychic to interpersonal analyses of behaviour, a shift begun by Adler in his quarrel with Freud. An analogous shift occurs from Pavlov to Skinner in experimental psychology, described in the second part of the book.

The fulcrum of the work is the part on Harry Stack Sullivan, for his interpersonal theory of personality represents the paradigmatic shift in its broadest terms. Following this, mechanisms rather than qualities of behaviour are considered in two chapters in which the basics of respondent and operant conditioning are described, along with their applications to psychodynamic psychologies, especially the interpersonal psychiatry of Sullivan. There is a final chapter on the unconscious after Freud, in which the emancipation of behaviourism from Watsonian dogma and Pavlovian reflexology are described. A concluding brief requiem addresses the question of the possible demise of systematic psychological science.

*

In creating this work out of chaos, I would like to acknowledge the assistance of Marilyn Weinper and Alison Balneaves who soldiered on through barricades of madness, and of numerous individuals over the years who (wittingly and unwittingly) gave me courage when the bottle looked empty. First among these I include Nancy Keehn, who must have suffered most.

PROEM

On Mind and Behaviour

Intrapsychic and transactional paradigms

Psychology literally means a discourse on the psyche, or mind, but it has always been concerned with two questions: the nature of consciousness and the causes of behaviour – that is, mind and will. Before Freud, it was common for these two questions to be treated as one, for traditional mental philosophers assumed that the causes of behaviour lay in consciousness, and that will is a property of mind. The nature of mind and the causes of behaviour have thus been regarded as one problem, not as two, on the assumption that the solution to the first question answers the second as well. The assumption may be symbolized $R = f(O)$, meaning that behaviour (R) is a function of events occurring inside the organism (O). Such a formulation adopts a 'self-action' approach to the causes of behaviour, as it takes these causes to reside in the behaving organism alone.[1] All that is necessary to explain its behaviour is to identify, or categorize, the organism. This is the sense in which terms such as 'introvert', 'schizophrenic', 'genius', or 'alcoholic' might be used as explanations of behaviour.

Whatever appeal action-type explanations may possess, they are patently not comprehensive. A person alone in an overheated apartment may decide to remove his or her clothing, and we may attribute the cause of this behaviour to that decision. A person likewise overheated in a crowded lecture hall would probably make a different decision. If the difference between the two decisions is explained by reference to differences between the two situations, then the type of explanation is no longer 'action' but 'interaction'. An interactional explanation of behaviour could be symbolized $R = f(O,S)$, meaning that behaviour (R) is a function of situational (S) as well as organismic (O) variables.

Both action-type and interaction-type explanations of behaviour fall within an S-O-R (stimulus-organism-response) paradigm[2] for psychology, for the paradigm presupposes that organismic events interpose between behaviour and the situations in which it occurs. In this paradigm, behaviour is typically regarded as a secondary datum that serves only to exemplify the workings of the mind, or some mental surrogate. Objectives of S-O-R psychology therefore involve *intrapsychic* analysis, for a complete understanding of the psyche supposedly provides a complete understanding of the behaviour it controls. Early forms of psychoanalysis and behaviourism fall within this paradigm, as does contemporary cognitive psychology.[3]

An alternative psychological paradigm appeals to transaction-type explanations of behaviour. In this case, control of an organism's behaviour is sought in the transactions between the organism and its environment: when an organism behaves, it causes a change in its environment, and the way in which the environment is changed itself maintains or modifies the behaviour of the organism.

The paradigm can be symbolized S-R-Sr (stimulus-response-reinforcement), where reinforcement (Sr) technically defines a particular environmental consequence that serves to maintain or strengthen behaviour (R) in some specifiable situation or stimulus (S). A transactional explanation of behaviour could be symbolized $RA = f(RB) = f(RA)$, meaning that the behaviour of person A (RA) is a function of the behaviour of person B (RB), which is a function of the behaviour of person A, etc. A common case in point is a conversation. An action-type explanation of an utterance is that a speaker says what is on his or her mind. But speeches are seldom made in the absence of a listener, so an interactional explanation appears to be required. However, a transactional analysis is helpful in accounting for the fact that typical conversations are non-linear. Later forms of psychoanalysis and behaviourism adopt this paradigm.[4]

The structure of the mind: the S-O-R paradigm

The S-O-R paradigm adopts, explicitly or implicitly, a number of doctrines from classical 19th-century mental philosophy.[5] These are dualism, structuralism, atomism, sensationism, associationism and rationalism.

- *Dualism* is the philosophical doctrine that there are two separate 'substances', body and mind. Belief in the second substance gives psychology its name – the study of the mind, or psyche. Psychology is therefore named after a theory, that mind exists to be studied, rather than after phenomenological or behavioural data.
- *Structuralism* is the doctrine that the mind can be specified according to its structure. It is the mental parallel to physical anatomy.
- *Atomism* is the doctrine that the structure of the mind can be reduced to a finite number of irreducible elements. It is the mental analogue of 19th-century atomic physics.
- *Sensationism* is the doctrine that the basic elements of mind are physical sensations – lights, sounds, smells, pressures, and tastes. These elements are not objects that are seen, heard, smelled, touched, or tasted, but the elementary attributes by which objects are known. They correspond to the table of elements in chemistry.
- *Associationism* is the doctrine that the wealth of human experience is composed of combinations of basic elementary sensations. The principal laws of combination, or association, debated by mental philosophers were those of contiguity, similarity, and contrast. These laws are the mental equivalents of the laws of combination of chemical elements.

Taken together, these doctrines define the programme for discovering the details of the S-O link of the S-O-R paradigm. The second, O-R, link was assumed to follow directly from the first, but in addition to its content acquired from the physical environment, the mind was supposed to be endowed with certain powers, or faculties, of its own.

- *Rationalism* is used here to encompass the notion that the human mind possesses a number of faculties, such as intellect, judgment, memory, reason, and will, by which it appreciates and evaluates a course of action that is freely chosen in a rational fashion. By this doctrine, the O-R link of the paradigm is added to the S-O link, and the complete S-O-R programme is explicated.

This programme is reasonable for psychology, provided that the fundamental doctrine of dualism is accepted. It has been challenged on a number of accounts, but it still provides the framework on which most of contemporary experimental psychology is built and out of which most mental health practices have developed.

Two minds: Freudian psychoanalysis

Several factors contributed to the demise of the classical conception that behaviour is controlled by a conscious mind endowed with powers of reason and will. One of the most important was the work of Sigmund Freud. Like many neurologists before him, Freud was confronted with patients with no apparent physical or intellectual impairment but whose behaviour nevertheless was non-rational and non-wilful. Their behaviour was different from normal, and Freud's first innovation was to suggest a novel answer to the question 'Different how?' Instead of assuming that abnormal behaviour was symptomatic of abnormally functioning consciousness, he assumed that all psychological phenomena are, in fact, lawful. He endeavoured to develop a psychological set of laws and principles that would encompass rational and irrational, voluntary and involuntary behaviour alike.

To this end, Freud worked out an elaborate structure for an unconscious mind. He postulated not one mind but two, a conscious mind acting in the conventional capacity as a repository for experience, and an unconscious mind responsible for the determination of action. The classical conception of a single mind that contained the phenomena of experience and that governed the initiation of behaviour was divided into a conception of two minds: a mind of experience and a mind of initiative. Freud's major interest was in the latter, but later contributions from some of his followers emphasized the former.

In spite of Freud's innovation, psychoanalysis remained within the classical S-O-R paradigm. It continued to consider behaviour merely as symptomatic of the workings of a mental apparatus. It proposed only a more elaborate apparatus than the one that had been proposed before, and it employed the method of association to explore the dynamics of this apparatus. Freud himself developed situational, organismic, and behavioural concepts within his system. Others offered different alternatives. In particular, the organismic (O) variable was elaborated by Jung, the situational (S) variable by Adler, and the behavioural (R) variable, with important changes, by Sullivan.

No minds: Watsonian behaviourism

By attributing the control of behaviour to an unconscious rather than to a conscious mind, Freud effectively disregarded the knowledge of consciousness in the explanation of behaviour. John B. Watson did the same, but for different reasons. Watson was a student of animal psychology, of organisms that were unable to introspect and communicate to him the contents of their conscious minds. He argued that such contents were not the subject-matter of psychology anyway, and established psychology as the study of behaviour. He eliminated the O from the S-O-R paradigm as a mental entity, thus founding so-called S-R psychology, or behaviourism.

Watson claimed behaviour as the datum of psychology, but his kind of methodological behaviourism did not, in fact, depart from the S-O-R paradigm. Instead, the mental O was replaced by a physical O. Where once behaviour was assumed to be explicable, given knowledge of mental content and function, the new assumption altered the arena of explanation from the mental to the physical. Despite appearances, Watson's behaviourism did not redeem its pledge to convert psychology to the scientific study of behaviour as such, for, as before, behaviour was taken only to index events occurring in another realm of analysis – that of neuroanatomy and physiology. The data and terminology taken to give substance to the behaviouristic programme were those of Pavlov, who was less interested in formulating a science of behaviour than in utilizing his conditioning methods to generate theories of cortical functions. These methods, like Freud's, were founded on the laws of association, but Pavlov focused on association by temporal contiguity, in contrast to Freud's insistence on association by significance.

Both Freud and Watson departed from tradition in accepting all behavioural phenomena as lawful and in rejecting the idea that consciousness controls behaviour. They each accepted, however, the convention of S-O-R psychology. They differed in that behaviourism replaced a conscious O by a physical one, and attended to quantitative measurements of behaviour, whereas psychoanalysis exchanged a conscious O for an unconscious one and offered more qualitative descriptions of characteristic human behaviours.

Transactional analysis: the S-R-Sr paradigm

Historically, from Freud to Watson, clinical developments in the S-O-R paradigm preceded those that emanated from the laboratory. The same historical order occurred in the origination and elaboration of S-R-Sr psychology, for the clinical elaboration of personality in interpersonal terms by Harry S. Sullivan was complete before the laboratory findings on the stimulus control of behaviour became understood as transactions between organisms and their environments. The new paradigm rests empirically on the Law of Effect, first stated by E.L. Thorndike in 1898 and later modified by B.F. Skinner and several others as technical and conceptual knowledge accrued.

Originally, the Law of Effect was used not to establish a new psychological paradigm but to buttress the traditional one, and it is still so used by a sizeable body of psychologists. The outstanding psychological system in the S-O-R paradigm based on the law of effect was that of C.L. Hull. Hull followed Watson in restricting his enquiries to observable stimulus and response data; he followed Freud in erecting an internal topography based upon them. In Hull's theory, effect, or reinforcement, serves to strengthen habits, which are major ingredients of the internal topographical system. The environment and the internal condition of the organism together are supposed to determine the behaviour of the organism. Although Hull acknowledged behaviour as the datum of psychology, the analysis of behaviour was not the objective of his theorizing. Like Freud and Watson, he continued to use behaviour only as an index of events occurring in an internal, O-variable, structure.

Skinner was the first practising experimental psychologist to establish the direct objective of psychology as the analysis of behaviour.[6] The Law of Effect made this programme possible because it is through response-reinforcement relationships that control of behaviour is acquired. In the simplest case, responses reinforced in one stimulus condition but not in another continue to occur in the first case but not in the second: stimulus control of a response is attained through differential reinforcement. The paradigm may be written S-R-Sr. The organism is not ignored, because it is an organism that is stimulated and its behaviour that is reinforced; but the focus of attention in the paradigm is on the relationship of the individual organism's behaviour to its environment, not on events occurring inside the organism's skin. The paradigm is holistic in a double sense – first, it is a whole organism that behaves, not parts of it (muscle twitches), and secondly, organism and environment are a unity, not one part within another.[7]

Radical behaviourism and psychoanalysis are alike in stressing the lawfulness of behaviour and the control of behaviour by unconscious events. They are unlike in that the former is interpersonal and quantitative while the latter is intrapsychic and qualitative. The quality of behaviour can be restricted in the laboratory but in the clinic it is the quality that is of first concern. This does not mean that the S-R-Sr paradigm is suitable in the laboratory and the S-O-R in the clinic, only that what can be created in the laboratory must be analysed in the clinic.

Psychoanalysis: contribution of clinical to general psychology

Whereas classical psychology was primarily concerned with the normal mind, and with mind-in-the-abstract rather than with particular individuals, and could contribute to abnormal psychology only by gratuitously postulating an abnormally structured or functioning mind, Freud developed both the theory and the therapy of psychoanalysis in the direct context of abnormal psychology, and then generalized his theory to include so-called normal personality functions.

Psychology took both its name and its subject-matter from an ancient belief in the duality of mankind. A live body is clearly different from a dead one, and the live body is commonly taken to be a dead one plus, or possessed by, a mind or soul. The live body appears to possess the attributes of initiative and consciousness over the dead one, and both these attributes are traditionally located in the mind – the same mind – the mind that classical psychology invested with faculties to account for its powers of initiative, and with an atomic substructure from which the complexity of conscious experience was formed. Freud divorced the mind of consciousness from the mind of initiative by locating the latter in the unconscious.[8]

Although the discovery of the unconscious is often counted as Freud's greatest achievement, this was subservient to his insistence upon psychological determinism, or functionalism, as it would now be called. He was not content to regard psychological phenomena as capricious, or accidental, but accepted the scientific faith that all phenomena are in one way or another functionally dependent upon antecedent events, however complex. The unconscious mental substructure that he invented – including the ego, the id, and the superego – was a means of bridging the gap between contemporary behaviour and its historical antecedents.

Freud's was the first important *functional science* of psychology.[9] He succeeded in showing that behaviour was not under the conscious control of mental faculties like will or reason – for the symptoms exhibited by his patients were neither willed nor reasonable – but depended upon certain specifiable incidents in their personal histories. However, although Freud was successful in showing *that* a person's behaviour was a function of his history, he did not show *how* this came about. What he did was to incorporate the history into the unconscious mind, with the result that psychoanalytic therapy concentrated on the analysis of the unconscious mind instead of on the means by which behaviour could be controlled and changed. Psychoanalysis, like classical psychology, assumes that if the mind is looked after, behaviour will take care of itself.

Behaviourism: contributions of general to clinical psychology

Like Freud, John B. Watson was dissatisfied with the classical psychology of his day. Watson was a comparative psychologist and found that he could continue his studies of animal behaviour without regard for the current controversies over the psychology of conscious experience, but instead of compounding an unconscious mental anatomy with a conscious one he legislated mentality out of psychology altogether. He defined the theoretical and practical goals of psychology, and insisted that the only logical and consistent *functional* psychology was behaviourism.

Watson's programme for a functional science of psychology did not require behaviourism to reject the whole concept of mind, only the mind of initiative, for in a functional science of behaviour the mind of initiative is irrelevant but the mind of consciousness is only uninteresting, technically speaking. Freud did not find the mind of consciousness interesting either, but he did not make the mistake of denying its existence. Watson did. Freud made a different mistake. He invented a mental substructure to mediate between the contemporary activities engaged in by a person and the historical events that appeared to determine them. Watson did not.

By discovering that contemporary behaviour could be related to past events, and that this relationship did not depend on consciousness, Freud showed that psychology could be lawful and non-mentalistic. He demonstrated that it could be a natural functional science with behaviour as its datum, a datum that varied in a comprehensible manner according to specifiable events in a life history. He could have developed a significant science of behaviour, but he did not. Instead, Freud compounded the mistakes of the Wundtian structuralists. In the place of one mind he substituted two, and the unconscious mind has proved to be as difficult to structure as the conscious mind.

In the place of historical and situational variables as controllers of behaviour, Freud substituted mental reifications in the form of the id, the ego and the superego. In the place of the simple statement that behaviour, R, is functionally dependent upon S, the biological and social history of the organism, the functional dependency was broken down to include O, the psychic substructure of the organism. But the fractionation of 'behaviour is a function of its antecedents' ($R = fS$) into 'behaviour is a function of the unconscious' ($R = fO$) and 'the unconscious is a function of its antecedents' ($O = fS$) is advantageous only if the sub-steps are amenable to independent investigation. But they are not. The O-variables introduced between behaviour and its antecedents have no independent functional existence – they can be manipulated only through S and made manifest only in R. As Jung has said, the unconscious really is unconscious. Watson's insistence that behaviourism is the only logical and consistent functionalism is an identical assertion. It is not so silly as the rejection of consciousness as a phenomenon of human experience, which he could not possibly have defended.[10]

Nevertheless, the early doctrine of behaviourism failed, partly because it could not carry the burden of its founder's apparent rejection of the mind of experience, but more importantly because Watson did not have the means to implement his functional programme. No more than Freud could he specify the way in which behaviour could be controlled, for the technical and conceptual innovations that Watson inherited from Pavlov proved inadequate for the development of a comprehensive science of psychology even within the boundaries that Watson had confined it. This inadequacy was remedied by B.F. Skinner. Out of his work and that of Pavlov grew the clinical technologies of behaviour therapy and behaviour modification.

Part I

Personality Dynamics

1

Freudian Psychodynamics

We inhabit a schizophrenic world that is also afflicted with multiple personality. There is, on the one hand, a markedly anti-Freudian atmosphere and, on the other, an effort by the American psychological establishment to ally itself with psychoanalysis.[1] Against this, we live in an era of deconstructionism that at the same time accepts or rejects psychoanalysis *in toto* as a world-view construct. In this and the following two chapters I shall elucidate psychoanalysis and other psychological systems in sufficient detail to permit the reader to deconstruct them and take or leave whatever elements he or she finds useful.

Psychoanalysis is both a general theory of human psychology and a psychotherapeutic technique, or, more properly, a group of theories and a set of techniques more or less directly developed by Sigmund Freud. Although Freud and his closest associates entered psychology by way of the medical sciences, there has been relatively little interaction between psychoanalysis and the experimental science of psychology, primarily because the majority of Freudian concepts are not amenable to investigation by traditional laboratory techniques. In addition, experimental psychology grew out of the classical philosophy of mentality and originally devoted itself to studies of the senses, which did not interest psychoanalysts.

On the other hand, psychoanalysis developed into a cultish society that became concerned with preserving its own existence, an attitude that does not appeal to experimentalists. Nevertheless, psychodynamics and the experimental analysis of behaviour do have some concepts in common, as subsequent chapters will display.

Fundamentals

The basic programme

In essence, psychoanalytic theory is *deterministic, non-rational, structural,* and *developmental.* Freud did not believe that mental events were capricious. He set out to give a functional account of such phenomena as dreams, slips of the tongue, blocked memories, hallucinations, and so on, that had previously been thought to be inexplicable or to occur at random.[2] Psychoanalytic theory was non-rational because it grew out of attention to phenomena that could not be explained in rational terms. Rational accounts could not be given of the contemporary behaviour exhibited by the hysterical, obsessional, paranoid, and phobic patients who consulted Freud, and the only alternative was to offer a non-rational explanation.

Freud's conception that behaviour has its causes was not particularly novel – other psychologists attributed human activity to causes, but these causes were taken to be rational, conscious mental faculties. Behaviour that could not be explained in these terms was not encompassed by academic psychology, and the crux of Freud's determinism was to extend the range of behavioural phenomena to which psychological science could apply. He did this by inventing a dynamic unconscious mind that incorporated a collection of forgotten incidents in an individual's lifetime.[3] This tactic alienated psychoanalysis from psychology, and was quite unnecessary from a functional point of view, although it did serve to add literary flesh to psychoanalysis over and above the bare bones of scientific behaviourism.

The developmental part of Freudian theory involves two aspects: the development of the structure of the unconscious and conscious minds, and the delineation of critical incidents, particularly weaning and toilet training, in the psychosexual development of the child. Untoward incidents occurring during these critical phases were supposed to plant blockages in the path of normal personality development, and the technical aspects of psychoanalysis were directed to the removal of these blockages to allow normal personality development to occur.

There are two sides to technical, therapeutic psychoanalysis:

analysis and synthesis. The objective of analysis is to break down a patient's resistances to the analyst's search for the roots of the psychological problems and expose the defences that maintain them. The important phase is that of *transference*, in which the patient transfers the source of his or her neurosis onto the therapist. During this phase the patient's past is brought into the present. The synthesizing process involves re-educating the patient so that his or her contemporary behaviour is related both to its historical antecedents and to the present circumstances; the control of behaviour is, so to speak, transferred from prior accidental events to the contrived events of the present reality. At this point the psychoanalyst is supposedly restructuring the patient's personality at a more mature level.

Although the theoretical and technical sides of psychoanalysis are intimately related, historically they are not entirely dependent upon each other. They are like basic and applied sciences, physics and engineering, for example. The discoveries of basic science require technical discoveries before they can be applied and, likewise, technical achievements can often pose problems for pure science. In the case of psychoanalysis, the basic scientific problems arose from technical practice – from applied science – and the basic 'pure' theories were developed initially in the wake of technical successes.

In fact, technical and theoretical developments in psychoanalysis have followed more or less definite stages: first the technical advances from hypnosis through suggestion to free association, then the theoretical modifications of the structure of the mental apparatus from the conscious, preconscious, unconscious to the ego, id, superego trilogy, and its development through psychosexual stages, then the further technical changes, not initiated by Freud, of brief analysis and supportive psychotherapy, which were concerned with showing up the defences of the ego instead of breaking them down, and last, the inclusion of non-conflict ego functions in the sphere of analytic theory.[4]

What is psychoanalysis?

It may seem strange to be asking what psychoanalysis is at this juncture, but the question is relevant because of the twofold (theoretical and technical) nature of psychoanalysis. It is possible to accept psychoanalytic theory in whole or in part without subscribing rigidly to its technical practices, and it is possible to utilize therapeutic techniques such as free association or dream analysis and interpretation without accepting Freudian theories. Early dissidents from Freudian theory, such as Jung, continued to use some of the technical practices emphasized by Freud, and quite radical technical innovations, for example brief psychotherapy or group therapy, may be used by reasonably orthodox theorists.

It is not always easy for the non-specialist to specify what separates modifications to Freudian therapy *within* psychoanalysis, like the developments of, say, Anna Freud, Hartmann, Kris, and Menninger, from the non-psychoanalytic systems of Adler, Horney, and Jung. The initial split in the psychoanalytic circle probably arose because personalities preceded principles,[5] and separate doctrines have since maintained the fragmentation of the original schools of dynamic psychotherapy. When Jung and Adler first broke away from Freud, they did so for reasons of theory, but psychoanalysis is now differentiated from analytic, individual and other schools of psychology on technical as well as on theoretical grounds. M.M. Gill, for example, said:

Psychoanalysis is that *technique* which, employed by a neutral psychoanalyst, results in the development of a *regressive transference neurosis* and the ultimate resolution of this transference neurosis by interpretation alone.[6]

Although this definition of psychoanalysis does make reference to a theoretical concept – regressive transference neurosis – the emphasis is plainly on technique, and the technical method is restricted to interpretation alone by a neutral analyst.

Freud, on the other hand, was more liberal and referred to psychoanalysis as

any line of investigation, no matter what its direction, which recognizes the two facts of *transference* and *resistance* and then takes them as the starting point of its work.[7]

So, apparently, Freud would not have insisted on a neutral therapist, in the sense of not interacting with his patient, or on therapy by interpretation alone, but only on the recognition of two facts. Insofar as Freud's facts are only theories to many other psychologists, Freud's claim is that psychoanalysis is principally a theory of psychology, a theory that rests on the twin concepts of transference and resistance.

Some basic theoretical concepts

Psychoanalysis may be said to have originated with Sigmund Freud's acquaintance with the 'talking cure' for 'hysteria'[8] used by Josef Breuer. Under hypnosis, patients would be taken back to earlier phases of their lives, and this sometimes resulted in an emotional catharsis and symptom removal.[9] The use of hypnosis for alleviating hysterical symptoms was used before Breuer and Freud by Janet, Charcot and others and dated back at least as far as Anton Mesmer, for whom Mozart wrote the short opera *Bastien and Bastienne*. But previous therapists had removed symptoms by suggestion, not, as Breuer and Freud did, by linking contemporary hysteria with the patients' personal history.

Just how successful Freud and Breuer were is difficult to say because there are relatively few published cases, and many of these are not particularly convincing to the uncommitted, as Freud knew. But some of the reported 'cures' were sufficiently dramatic to make it appear that hysterias could be traced to early experiences. That behaviour (R) is a function of historical situations (S) can be taken as having been demonstrated by Freud. He and Breuer were able to make sense of behaviour that earlier psychologists could not explain. Freud gave a non-rational account of behaviour and populated an unconscious mind with irrational elements that initiate behaviour. He expanded the discovery that R depends on S into the theory that R depends on O and O depends on S, where O is an unconscious mental apparatus of greater or lesser complexity. Psychoanalytic theory then proceeded to develop each of these variables, S, O and R, in turn, although principal attention was directed to the O-variable, the structure of the 'unconscious mind'.

The O-variable

Topographical structure

The earliest Freudian structuralization of the mind was into three levels: conscious, pre-conscious, and unconscious. The conscious mind was taken to hold those mental contents currently in awareness, and differed from the pre-conscious, which is supposed to be the repository of latent thoughts and feelings that are not in immediate awareness but that can easily become so.

Both conscious and preconscious levels of mentality are purely descriptive: some things are in awareness at any given instant and other things are not, but they can be recollected when required. But there are, according to Freud, other mental events that are barred from consciousness under normal circumstances, and these he located in the unconscious. The unconscious was invented to explain behaviour, not just to describe certain facts of experience. It is a theoretical invention designed to bridge the gap between contemporary behaviour and its historical origins. Its status is like that of the ether in classical physics or the memory in traditional psychology except that it is active (dynamic), not just a passive medium of transmission.

The material in the unconscious is supposedly forced there out of consciousness by means of *repression*, and is held there by a barrier that resists its return to awareness.[10] Transmission from the unconscious to the conscious mind is possible only under special circumstances, such as when the individual is dreaming or free-associating. But mental events that reach consciousness in this way do so in disguised form, and the function of the psychoanalyst is to penetrate this disguise and interpret it to the patient.

Experimental demonstrations of learning without awareness do not bear on the unconscious as conceived by Freud because the Freudian unconscious contains repressed material, not material which just happened to go unnoticed. There are experimental examples of learning without awareness, but they do not invoke the concept of repression.[11] The circumstances to which the Freudian unconscious refers require a distinction to be made between motor learning and verbal learning; not just a distinction in kind, but a recognition that one can take place in the absence of the other.[12]

This is plainly seen in young children who do many things before they learn to talk, and in older children who often cannot say why they are engaging in some activity, and in alcoholic blackouts.

Freud himself agrees that an event becomes conscious 'through becoming connected with the word-presentations corresponding to it',[13] and the objective of psychoanalysis is to make this connection, but it does not follow that the verbal behaviour has been repressed and somehow causes the motor behaviour. It is equally possible that the verbal accompaniment to the motor activity may not have been learned in the first place.

By postulating repression rather than the lack of learning as the mechanism that populated the unconscious mind, Freud was forced also to invent a repressing force, and reasons why repression takes place. This was accomplished by differentiating mentality into a number of functional energy systems.

Functional differentiation

Once analytic theory became committed to the notion of an unconscious mind that really existed it was forced to complicate this mind by adding other elements in addition to repressed material into the unconscious mind.

This complication was forced upon Freud by his analytic practice, but part of the solution was taken from outside psychoanalysis. This was his acceptance of the id, as postulated by Georg Groddeck.[14] The id, or 'it', was Groddeck's name for the psychological energizer that activated an otherwise passive self, as an automobile's engine drives its chassis. Freud invested the id with instinctual motivating forces and placed it in the unconscious mind. In fact, it *was* the mind of the infant. This set of instinctual forces he assumed to be immutable. They were entirely selfish and unaffected by the consequences of the acts it initiated.

The ego was now taken to develop out of the id as a result of the individual's contact with reality. It was the ego that gained or suffered according to the results of id-initiated behaviour. By virtue of its relation to the outer world the ego is conscious, but its roots were taken to lie in the unconscious mind. In this way a solution was offered to the problem of how to make the ego partly conscious and partly unconscious, a problem created by the resistance of a patient to an analyst's interpretations in therapy (see below).

Also in the unconscious are those wishes repressed by the ego, and these repressed wishes can only reach consciousness in the service of the id. The conscious ego must respond to the demands of reality – it develops according to what Freud called the *reality principle*. But the id is not the servant of reality; it is governed by the *pleasure principle*. The id reacts entirely hedonistically, and so long as the behaviour it instigates in the ego does not result in adverse reactions from the outside world, ego and id act in harmony. But when the id forces the ego into conflict with reality, conditions are created for a struggle between the ego and the id, resulting in the ego defending itself by repression and other defence mechanisms described below.

Freud invested the ego with control of the so-called motor apparatus and also of the perceptual system. It is the ego that experiences the external world (through the perceptual system) and directs the individual's behaviour towards it (through the motor apparatus). But it is the id that provides the psychic energy. The id is the engine and the ego the steering mechanism and neither can act without the other, except insofar as the engine drives along purely instinctual paths, particularly those of sex and aggression. However, these instincts, being entirely selfish, are likely to bring the individual quickly into conflict with social reality, for which the ego must suffer. Consequently the ego may not use the motor apparatus solely according to the wishes of the id.

The action of the ego on the motor apparatus to gratify libidinal id needs is known as the *primary process*; the reflective, cognitive assessment of the possible effects of different courses of action is called the *secondary process*. If the id gratification is impossible, the primary process may effect distortions in the perceptual system, such as hallucinations and misperceptions.

Ego psychology

One of the more significant developments within psychoanalysis that did not originate with Sigmund Freud has amplified the ego beyond its role in the dynamic resolution of conflicts. Heinz Hartmann refers to this additional portion of the ego as the 'conflict-free ego sphere'. Within this conflict-free sphere of the ego, or the rational ego, are included the traditional higher mental processes such as abilities, intelligence, memory and other cognitive skills that assist in adaptation.

The objective of ego psychology, as it is called, is to extend psychoanalysis into the whole field of general psychology. From the point of view of ego psychology, only part of the ego develops as a result of conflicts with reality (by reality testing), the remainder resulting from cognitive maturation in the way that, for example, intelligence is often supposed to develop. This portion of the ego is taken to be inherited and not to grow out of the id as the Freudian ego does.[15]

According to orthodox psychoanalytic ego theory there is no truly adaptive behaviour, only defensive behaviour which, by Hartmann's account, is 'ego limiting'; the rational ego supplies the means for intelligent avoidance of real environmental dangers. This conception of an expanded ego also has technical implications, because before traditional analysis is undertaken (to break down the ego defences in order to clarify the libidinal forces underlying a particular neurotic syndrome) the strength of the ego to reconstitute itself adaptively must first be determined. Without sufficient ego strength to begin with, it might not be possible to re-synthesize an ego that had been stripped of its ordinary, even if neurotic, defences. In such a case analysis would not be recommended.[16]

Another component of the Freudian psyche is the superego. It is the moral aspect of personality – 'thou shalt not' in contrast 'to thou canst not'. Whereas ego is taken to develop out of the organism's direct contact with the physical world, what Skinner calls contingency controlled behaviour, the superego is a function of its relationship to the psychological world – the control exercised by people rather than by inanimate objects. It is the individual's indirect contact with the physical world through the mores of society (Skinner calls this rule-governed behaviour) instead of through the actual results of his or her behaviour. The major part of the superego develops after the emergence of the ego, principally during the Oedipal period (see below), but part of it must exist from the beginning in the form of the repressing part of the ego.

The superego, or ego-ideal, is incorporated into the personality through the mechanisms of *introjection* and *identification*.[17] According to analytic theory the infant boy has sexual designs on his mother and sees himself as the rival of his father whom he wishes to kill and marry his mother, as Oedipus (unwittingly) did in Sophocles' play. Such, the analytic story goes, is the strength of the Oedipal desire that the ego alone is not sufficient to repress it, and extra strength is gained by identification with the father, and introjection of his values into the child. These introjected values are the essence of the superego, which becomes a third force that struggles with reality and the id for command, through the ego, of the motor apparatus. How the individual behaves depends upon the resolution of the three-way id-reality-superego struggle. However the Freudians do not attend to behaviour as such, but to the mechanisms by which the ego defends itself during the conflict. These mechanisms are called the mechanisms of defence.

The R-variable

Psychoanalysis is never concerned with behaviour as a subject matter in its own right, but only as it represents the expression of the interplay of underlying psychic forces. Nevertheless, the results of these subterranean interactions have been elaborated into kinds of behaviour, particularly *ego defence mechanisms* and *resistances*.

The defence mechanisms are the systems of behaviour adopted by the ego (through its control of the motor apparatus) to maintain the integrity of the organism in everyday life, and if the result of these defences is the production of neurotic symptoms, the task of the analyst is to trace the origins of the conflict or conflicts that the ego is defending against, to discover the kinds of defences used, and to reconstitute the personality by expunging the conflict so that more adaptive behaviour can emerge.[18] Resistances are the kinds of behaviour adopted by the analysand during analytic sessions in which the mechanisms of defence are in the process of breaking down (see below).

As Anna Freud points out in *The Ego and the Mechanisms of Defence*, although psychoanalytic *theory* has been largely id-dominated (through its concentration on the dynamics of motivation) psychoanalytic *therapy* is necessarily ego-centered. It is the ego that is 'sick', that has failed in its relations with the world, and it is the ego that must return to cope with reality once the reasons for its

failure have been discovered. The reason that a person seeks psychotherapy, she argues, is that the ego has failed to defend itself in
one way or another, and has not successfully adapted to the demands made of it; thus it is to the ego that psychoanalysis is
basically directed. The reason she gives for rejecting hypnosis as a
psychoanalytic technique in favour of free association is that in
hypnosis the ego is 'forcibly restrained'. This forcible restraint
allows id impulses to appear unmodified by the ego, and therefore
behaviour under hypnosis neither indicates how the ego operates
nor allows ego and id energies to integrate. Free association, on the
other hand, is conceived as only *persuading* the ego from interfering
with id wishes as they appear, and leaving the ego sufficiently
unrestrained to come to grips with these wishes.

Free association is known as the fundamental rule in psychoanalytic therapy. The patient is instructed to relax and say
everything that comes to mind, no matter how foolish, embarrassing, or irrelevant it appears to be. This is an extraordinarily difficult
rule to follow but it also has another aspect: free association applies
only to verbal, not to motor behaviour. The psychoanalytic fundamental rule requires the analysand to *say* everything that occurs to
him or her, but not to *do* anything. The analysand is forbidden to
'act out' the id impulses that are released into consciousness. Consequently there is no id gratification during free association.
Libidinal forces appear as verbal behaviour, but control of the
motor apparatus is retained by the ego. This control is lost under
hypnosis, says Anna Freud.

However, the appearance of the id in verbal behaviour is, by
Anna Freud's account, modified by unconscious defence processes.
The unconscious ego is not directly revealed by free association but
shows itself through its effects on the id. The assumption is that id
wishes would be easily recognizable in their direct form – that is,
they would be verbalized as undisguised sexual or aggressive statements. As they are deflected defensively from these areas by the
unconscious component of the ego, this part of the ego has to be
deduced through analysis.

Within the theory it must be the unconscious ego that disguises
the id, because the id, working by the primary (non-intellectual)
process, cannot disguise itself. Any modification of direct id statements, therefore, must be accomplished by the unconscious ego.

The situation is reduced to a single equation with a single unknown, the functioning of the unconscious ego, and it is the solution of the equation that is the first objective of psychoanalysis, according to Anna Freud. The possible solutions are available in the form of defence mechanisms, which classify the kinds of behaviour that are important in psychoanalytic theory. It is in the sense that these mechanisms are functional classes of behaviour that they may be regarded as the elaboration of the R-variable within psychoanalysis.

Ego defences and their manifestations

Of the many forms of ego defence, pride of place goes to *repression*. In fact, at first it was the only defence. It was *the* way in which the unconscious was populated, and bridged the gap between contemporary behaviour and its historical antecedents in a person's life. It was taken to be the defence utilized in hysteria, the disorder that provided the original data for psychoanalytic theory.

Repression is not a class of behaviour, but the absence of behaviour. Its action is deduced if normal sexual and aggressive impulses, as hypothesized by libido theory, are weak, distorted or absent. Repression is taken to be a permanent defence mechanism, and its action is only observable during neurotic ego disintegration. It is a debilitating process because part of the libidinal energy is blocked – like a motor-car running on three cylinders – and part of this energy is also required to do the blocking. This latter is known as anticathexis, the direction of energy flowing back into the id instead of outward from it.

Freud himself distinguished two aspects of repression, primal repression and repression proper.[19] Primal repression refers to the exclusion of libidinal wishes from consciousness and to the fixation of the relevant libidinal energy. As such, primal repression results only in a loss of psychic energy, with a consequent reduction in behaviour output. Repression proper is the conscious affect, particularly anxiety, resulting from primal repression.

Repression is an unconscious denial by the ego of impulses from the id, and its operation is assumed when appropriate instinctual behaviour is absent. But Anna Freud has attributed two particular kinds of behaviour to id denial – denial in fantasy, and denial in word and act. Fantasy is a form of ego defence in which fantasized greatness and success serve to deny failures in actuality, and denial in word or act are ways of bolstering the ego by self-reassurance or bravado.

In an early paper on instincts and their vicissitudes, Sigmund Freud went beyond the notion of mere denial of instincts to their actual reversal, or turning round upon the subject.[20] This paper antedated the elaboration of the ego defence mechanisms and was concerned with alterations in the instincts themselves. This kind of reversal Anna Freud refers to as *turning against the self*; it is when the instinct takes its own ego as its object, so that love is directed into exhibitionism, aggression into masochism, and so on. This is a *reversal of aim* of the instinct.

A second form of reversal is *reversal of content* of the instinct from, say, hate into love, a mechanism also known as *reaction formation*. Reaction formation looks like 'normal', as against defensive, ego development, except for possible indications of obsessional exaggerations and occasional lapses or reversals, such as the doting mother who severely punishes her child for some trivial offence.

A more general example of the defensive alteration of the aim of an instinct is *displacement*. Displacement before Freud was described by Sheridan in *The Rivals*, Act II, Scene i, where Fag, the servant, is chastised by his master, Captain Absolute, just after the captain had been scolded by his father, Sir Anthony Absolute. Fag remarks, 'Soh! Sir Anthony trims my master. He is afraid to reply to his father – then vents his spleen on poor Fag! – When one is vexed by one person, to revenge one's self on another, – who happens to come in the way – is the vilest injustice.' In this case, in Freud's language, the instinct is directed onto a socially acceptable object instead of onto one that would bring social approbation. A related mechanism is *isolation*, referring to the isolation of the id from its object. The libidinal impulse is said to enter consciousness and control the motor apparatus through the ego, but the object of the impulse is changed and the affect is divorced from its initial objective.

When displacement is socially productive, the defence is called *sublimation*. Sexual libido is for procreation – creative production – and any form of artistic or other creative activity is traced by the psychoanalysts to sublimated libidinal energies. This account of the procreative source of creativity has been lampooned on the ground that creative artists do not exhibit marked lack of normal potency, but according to Anna Freud, sublimation does not necessitate less direct sexual activity, for 'the drives which normally contribute most to sublimation are not the genital sex urge, but its primitive pregenital components which are for the most part excluded from fulfilment when normal adult genitality has set in'.[21]

However, artistic creativity has also been attributed to another defence mechanism, *regression*. Regression is the return to an earlier form of successful behaviour in the face of a current danger. The child who is overwhelmed by fear might cry out 'Mother!' and be comforted. The soldier wounded in battle might let out the same cry. But to be successful as a defence of the ego's self-esteem the earlier successful behaviour must be applicable to the contemporary situation, and as this is seldom the case regressive behaviour is usually neurotic, or even psychotic. But not all regression need be bad, and regression can sometimes take place 'in the service of the ego'. When regression results in childlike autistic loosening of thought the result may be psychosis but it may also release the imagination from the constraints of social conditioning so that genuine creativity of thought can occur.[22] Via regression, then, psychoanalysis links creativity with madness.[23]

Projection is one of the best known Freudian defence mechanisms because of its association with projective tests, although many psychological tests that are classified as projective have only the slenderest connection with the defence mechanism as conceived by Freud. There are several varieties of projection,[24] not all of which are necessarily ego-defensive. For example, misperceptions of the objective world according to the prevailing needs and feelings of an individual has been called projection, but this is not the sense in which Freud used the term.

As a psychoanalytic defence mechanism, projection goes hand in hand with denial – libidinal impulses are said to be denied by the ego and at the same time attributed to another person or object. The man who is angry with his wife for burning his breakfast toast may repress his own anger and in all honesty ask her why she is in such an ugly mood that morning. Her reply might be denial, or acting out by throwing the coffee pot!

Freudian projection does involve misperception, of course, but it is not merely misperception that exemplifies projection; it is that the misperception frees the individual from shame or guilt over the possession of socially unacceptable impulses. Although Freud did in fact allow that good as well as bad impulses could be projected this is not projection in the service of ego defence. Projection in this case, according to the Dutch existential psychiatrist, J. Van den Berg, is a fact of an individual's being – 'while telling us what his world looked like, he tells us without prevarication, without any mistake, how he is himself'.[25] This is the inward revealed outwardly but it is not necessarily defensive; it is just as likely to reveal peoples' good as their bad points.

Writing in 1951, Anna Freud limited the importance of successful projection to childhood. She says in her book:

> Projection, in the psychoanalytic sense of the word, is an ego mechanism which normally occurs early in infantile life and, for a while, plays an important part in governing the child's relationship with the environment. It loses this role when other important mechanisms come into play, ... In later life projection again plays an important part in pathological states, such as paranoia (p. 485).

This placement of projection in a developmental context bears some resemblance to Harry Stack Sullivan's conception of *parataxia*, which is discussed in Chapter 3.

Two fairly similar ego defensive reactions are *rationalization* and *undoing*. Earlier reference has been made to rationalization as the learned verbal accompaniment to acquired motor behaviour. Motor behaviour is usually attributed to ideational (mental) activity; traditionally, verbal behaviour is regarded as merely the means of making the mental activity public. Freud reversed the usual order and argued that behaviour frequently does not occur for the reasons given, but that the verbalizations are rationalizations invented after the act to satisfy social inquiry and to maintain self-esteem.

Rationalization is excusing, undoing is apologizing. In both cases the motor apparatus, governed by the ego, has performed a destructive instinctual act. But, in the first case, responsibility for the act is denied, while in the second, it is regretted, by apologies or offers of retribution.

The ego may defend itself by seeking alliance with the superego (see below). Such a means of defence is *identification with the aggressor*. In this case the ego is said to introject into itself the qualities of the object that frustrates libidinal satisfaction. This can occur in play, or during the resolution of the Oedipal situation as noted above. Alternatively, a defensive arrangement may be made with reality in the sense that the ego's activities are reduced to the extent of avoiding situations that create frustration and anxiety.

All of these mechanisms are either forms of motor behaviour, in the gross sense, or statements made about motor behaviour. They can be accounted for in the terms of behaviour theory either as activities that derive reinforcement from the physical environment directly or that are acceptable to (reinforced by) other people. Thus, the child who offends either its parents or its peers comes to learn how to account for its transgressions in ways that satisfy those it has trespassed against. It is unlikely that behaviourists would have come to specify these ways as fluently or as quickly as the Freudians, for their approach is by way of synthesizing the complex from the simple rather than by direct analysis of complicated behaviour.

A somewhat different form of defence mechanism is *symbolism*, one of the mechanisms employed by Freud in deriving the latent from the manifest content of a dream. It is a mechanism whereby dream images avoid direct expression of socially unacceptable wishes or acts. As expressed by Ernest Jones in his *Papers on Psychoanalysis*, symbols serve to disguise events, in contrast to adjectives, which describe them literally, similes, which describe them comparatively, and metaphors, which reify them.

Anxiety and defence

The ego's motives for defending against instincts have been elaborated in Anna Freud's book, to which I have already referred. The opposing forces that are drawn into conflict for control of the ego are the id, reality, and the superego. It is the various alliances of these forces according to circumstances that determine the ego's motives for defence. So far the discussion has presupposed primarily an ego-id conflict, but this is obviously limited because frequently there would be no reason for the ego to resist the id. It is only when superego and reality factors resist the ego's direct expression of libidinal impulses that the ego is forced to struggle against the id.

Anna Freud distinguishes three kinds of anxiety that call for defence, and these kinds of anxiety depend on whether the ego is threatened by the superego, reality or the id. *Superego anxiety*, found in adult neurosis, is the case where it is the superego that resists the id, and where ego and superego combine to prevent direct instinctual expression. This is the classical example given by Sigmund Freud of the production of neurotic anxiety as a result of over-strict childhood training. It is the direct opposite of a later position taken by O.H. Mowrer, that neurosis is caused by insufficient superego training.[26]

Objective anxiety is said to occur when the ego and reality join forces against the id. This can happen through parental prohibitions, threats, and actual punishment, as against moralizing and appealing to the conscience of the child. By threats and punishments for instinctual behaviour, fears are instilled into the child, giving anxiety generated by libidinal feelings a genuinely objective basis.

Thirdly, *instinctual anxiety* refers to a direct ego-id confrontation, as when the potency, or 'impetus', of the id threatens to overwhelm the ego. Sexual feelings at puberty would provide such an instance of an unprepared ego fairly suddenly faced with controlling an exceptionally powerful id. Instinctual anxiety only becomes intelligible if instincts as energies are distinguished from their concomitant affects. Sexual feelings are not unpleasant so there would be no reason for the ego to defend against them unless objective or superego anxiety were also present. But it is the instinct as such that is supposedly defended against, regardless of the quality of the accompanying affect.

Implications for therapy

Neurosis is a behavioural manifestation of ego defences, according to psychoanalytic theory, and the objective of psychoanalytic therapy is to encourage a transference neurosis through which the defences will be revealed to the therapist. So, for example, if guilt feelings emerge during analysis, then defence against the superego is assumed, whereas the appearance of objective fear or anxiety is taken to reveal defence against reality.

One characteristic claimed for psychoanalytic technique, it will be remembered, is the therapist's neutrality. But the therapist is not neutral, he or she as the case may be is, supposedly, passive. And this passivity necessarily frustrates the patient, for none of the superficial, learned, defensive methods of dealing with social interactions work. Consequently the patient tries a variety of tactics to obtain a reaction from the psychiatrist, and it is these tactics that reveal the successively more significant layers of a patient's personality.

A succinct and amusing description of psychoanalytic treatment from the patient's point of view is related by Karl Menninger:[27]

> With half a laugh of hearty zest
> I strip me off my coat and vest
>
> Then heeding not the frigid air
> I fling away my underwear
>
> So having nothing else to doff
> I rip my epidermis off
>
> More secrets to acquaint you with
> I pare my bones to strips of pith
>
> And when the exposé is done
> I hang, a cobweb skeleton
>
> While you sit there aloof, remote
> And will not doff your overcoat.

Resistances

Resistances are also defences, but they are defences of the neurosic *status quo*. They are the defences put up by patients in opposition to the analysis of their normal ego defences. A non-technical account of his own resistances in a nine-year course of psychoanalysis is given by Sydney Poitier in his autobiography, *This Life*.

Psychoanalysis recognizes that neurotic behaviour is functional, so ego resistance to analysis is to be expected. Although they use different theoretical languages, psychoanalysts and functional behaviourists agree that behaviour becomes consolidated if it deals effectively with the environment. Behaviour is said to defend the ego in the one case and to be reinforced in the other. Neurosis is not maladaptive as such, but is a maladaptive epiphenomenon, as it were, of adaptive behaviour. Stealing, for example, is adaptive for the hungry child who wants bread and cannot get it any other way, but it has neurotic overtones if the adult feels chronically guilty because of stealing as a child. The adult visits the psychiatrist because of the maladaptive side of his or her personality, but resistance to analysis results from the possible disruption of the adaptive side of personality. Resistances are said to have sources in the ego, id, and superego and to take many forms.[28] Ego resistances, that is resistances to analysis by the ego, include *epinosic gain resistance*, *transference resistance*, and *repression resistance*. The first of these refers to the stealing example just discussed. Freud called the functional side of neurosis *secondary gain*; epinosic gain resistance describes the resistance put up by the ego to loss of secondary gain.

Transference resistance has its source in the passivity of the therapist, as mentioned above. The patient presumably enters therapy with some expectations from his or her experiences in everyday life, but when these expectations are not fulfilled, insofar as the patient gives money and time but gets nothing in return, negative transference, the transference of negative affect to the therapist, is likely to occur. In this case the patient may criticize the therapist, question his or her competence, and terminate treatment. When this happens the psychoanalyst attributes the patient's behaviour to transference resistance; meanwhile the educated patient sees this explanation as a defence of the *therapist's* ego! There are no rules in psychoanalytic theory for deciding who is right, but the problem seldom arises because one of the contestants is also the referee.

Repression resistance is said to occur when the ego resists the appearance in consciousness of repressed negative affect such as fear, guilt, or anxiety during analysis. Hysterical neurosis is not marked by conscious feelings of anxiety; in fact, it was characterized by Janet as 'la belle indifference', and insofar as the ego is defended by repression of unpleasant feelings it resists the overcoming of repression during analysis.

A form of resistance supposedly adopted by the id is *repetition compulsion*. Repetition compulsion refers to the recurrence in a variety of ways during an individual's life of manifestations of critical early traumatic incidents.[29] The transference neurosis that is the climax of psychoanalysis is such an event. Insofar as the id is responsible for these recurrences, and that transference sets the occasion for cure, it is the id that would resist exposure, by the device of changing the form of the neurotic appearance of the repetition compulsion. An example is a case reported by Anna Freud of a young woman who, at successive stages of analysis, first exhibited hatred for her mother, then displaced this hatred onto another female, then turned the hatred against herself and finally, convinced she was being persecuted, projected her hatred onto other women.

A patient's claim that he or she really is guilty, to deserve to suffer, is taken by Karl Menninger as resistance on the part of the superego. Anna Freud regards such claims as signs that the original defence was against superego anxiety. O.H. Mowrer, on the other hand, believes that feelings of guilt are an essential part of neuroses, and that cure is affected when the patient manages to atone for this guilt in one way or another. The importance of guilt is also recognized by Albert Ellis,[30] who claims that the neurotic generalizes guilt over particular occurrences to a total feeling of unworthiness. The patient reasons, so to speak: 'I have been guilty. Therefore, I am unworthy.' Ellis uses so-called rational therapy to teach the patient the falsity of his logic. Neither Mowrer nor Ellis would regard acceptance of guilt as evidence of superego resistance, but these men are not members of the psychoanalytic profession and do not practice psychoanalysis, although Ellis did at one time.

Acting-out is another method of resistance mentioned by Menninger. It will be remembered that the fundamental rule of psychoanalysis requires free association in words, not actions, so that direct motor expression of emotion breaks the rule. Acting-out is a resistance in this sense. In the early days of psychoanalysis, and in later applications to drug therapy, the explosion into activity of repressed emotions was taken to be required for cure, but later emphasis on ego analysis in place of id analysis has changed this view in the interests of theoretical consistency.

Finally, when patients appear to enjoy analysis and to do all they can to please the therapist, they are said to be engaging in *erotization resistance*. Menninger relates the behavioural manifestations of erotization resistance to the stages of psychosexual development (see below). When the patient talks too much, or succeeds in manipulating the analyst into doing a great deal of talking, the patient may be resisting the progress of analysis at the oral stage. If too much encouragement is needed and the patient 'strains' hard to produce, then the resistance is anal. Overindulgence in sexual fantasies (what is the limit of normal indulgence?) means resistance at the phallic and genital stages, according to whether the fantasies are narcissistic or seductive, respectively.

So, the theory goes, in daily life, the patient behaves in neurotic ways and these ways exemplify the workings of ego defences. In analysis, the patient behaves in other ways and these ways are resistances to the analysis of the defences. The patient strips bare, so to speak, and the analyst sits there all bundled up in a spidery web of theory.

The S-variable

Freud believed that events in a life history critically determine how a personality will develop, but he did not regard all events as equally significant. Once again it was not the historical events themselves that interested Freud but the effect they had on the developing libido. Historical-situational variables enter into psychoanalytic theory because they provide different objects onto which the libido can fasten as the individual matures. They enter into Sullivan's interpersonal psychiatry as stages in relationships with significant others, and into Skinner's radical behaviourism as sources of reinforcement.

A more complete picture of the relevance of S-variables to psychoanalysis can be seen by reference to Freud's theory of neurosis. There are four ingredients that go to make up this theory: frustration, regression, libidinal fixation, and intrapsychic conflict. Frustration is taken to be the immediate, contemporary, precipitating cause of neurosis. The frustrating situation itself may be largely accidental, but what is not accidental is the condition of the personality that is frustrated. The dynamic effect of frustration is regression; the libido retreats to an earlier stage in its development, meaning that in the present it utilizes energy fastened onto objects at some earlier time. This earlier time is the time at which the libido fixated due to certain traumatic experiences in particular situations during childhood. If in addition there is intrapsychic conflict, the result is neurosis; otherwise the individual may exhibit a perverted character, but would not be categorized as neurotic.[31]

The important element in this mixture so far as the S-variable is concerned is libidinal fixation. This is what is supposed to occur if critical life incidents are not properly overcome. Freud conceived of the sexual libido as developing through a succession of organizational levels, which he compared to the progress of a migrating people. At selected points, he imagined, these people would leave behind some of their number to set up and organize staging encampments, and these would be 'prepared positions' to which the main body could fall back in case of threat.

The 'migrating people' constitute the libido, and the staging encampments the organization of the libido around certain erogenous zones on its journey to maturity. The strongest organization that the libido leaves behind is the developmental level at which it is said to be fixated. It is the level to which it regresses when danger threatens. This is the essence of the theory of psychosexual development, which itself specifies the kinds of events likely to result in libidinal fixation, and the kinds of personalities that develop accordingly.

Psychosexual development

Freud conceived of the libido as organizing itself successively in the course of human growth around three erogenous zones: mouth, anus and genitals. The transition from zone to zone with increasing age was thought to be biologically determined, but the effects of situational factors are felt because improper childhood training practices (from the psychoanalytic point of view) may fixate the libido and thereby interfere with its normal development. These practices have been elaborated by Freud himself, particularly with regard to toilet training and the 'anal character',[32] and by K. Abraham[33] and Edward Glover[34] with respect to weaning. In addition, Otto Rank[35] has argued for the importance of the conditions surrounding birth – the birth trauma – as a determinant of personality.

The libido is supposed to advance to mature genitality through a series of pre-genital stages, the first of which is the *oral phase*, when sexuality is concentrated around the mouth. At this time the infant is passive and dependent, all its needs being met by an attendant adult with the principal need being satisfied by ingestion of food through the mouth. Thus the source of libidinal gratification is in the oral region.

The important situational variable at this point is the way in which the infant is fed – by bottle or by breast. Breast-feeding is preferred by psychoanalysts because it provides for a warm and comforting mother onto whom the libido can fasten. The more general aspects of the presence or absence of the mother have been stressed by Rene Spitz and Margaret Ribble, among others, who claim to have demonstrated fairly gross personality and intellectual defects, even to the point of death, in infants weaned away from their mothers.

However, these findings, in particular those reported by Spitz, have been severely challenged on a number of grounds,[36] although work on infant monkeys directed by Harry Harlow at the University of Wisconsin Primate Laboratory has shown that cuddling and rocking are critical maternal responses necessary for a high survival rate of monkey offspring.[37] Moreover, those animals successfully and artificially reared without normal mothering turned out to be deviant and incompetent when it came to rearing their own young, or even in engaging in sexual behaviour. However, not all early defects were irreversible.[38]

When the infant gets a little older, it passes from the oral passive to the oral sadistic stage. This is the time when the first teeth begin to appear, and also includes the time of weaning. Oral sadism refers to the fact that the infant begins to bite the breast that feeds it, although it is recognized that biting may be occasioned by physical maturation and irritation of the gums with no sadistic intent. The weaning situation is an important one for psychoanalysis, for it is an obvious occasion on which frustrating conflicts can occur, although different accounts of the conflict have been given by different analysts. The more orthodox account refers to an internal conflict between love and hate. Love is the normal reaction when the libido is gratified by the breast, but the withdrawal of the love object at weaning is said to lead to hate and so set the occasion for oral sadistic behaviours. Other accounts refer more directly to the frustrating effects of the weaning as such on the gratification of the oral need. Thus Karl Abraham claims that fixation may occur either if the oral need is not satisfied (because the child is weaned too early) or if the need becomes overindulged by weaning at too late an age. Those children whose supposed need for sucking is met are referred to as orally gratified types, while those whose sucking need is not gratified are classified as orally ungratified. Ungratified babies are the ones who resort to biting in the oral sadistic stage, or so the theory goes.

These types, Abraham believes, grow into two different types of adults, which he characterizes in terms of the condition of the infant during weaning. Thus the infant who is orally gratified is one whose needs have been met and who has successfully encompassed a change in feeding habits. Such a child is said to grow into an optimistic, sanguine, generous, and sociable adult. The orally ungratified child, on the other hand, as an adult would be pessimistic, surly, insecure, sensitive to criticism, and depressed. The adult personality characteristics are drawn by analogy with the hypothesized reaction of the child, and the weaning situation with which the child was confronted is taken to be the cause of its personality as an adult. This is not an implausible hypothesis, but is difficult to test in individual cases. There are some indications of a correlation between time of weaning and adult personality along the lines that Abraham suggests,[39] but the relationship is not necessarily functional, or causal.

The next level of libidinal organization is at the *anal stage*, and the important situation here is toilet training. This is apparently the first point at which Freud seriously considered psychic development from the standpoint of interpersonal relationships. Here was seen the first attempt by the mother to train the child to conform to the expectations of society. Freud emphasized both major libidinal components – sexuality and aggression – at this stage, sexuality being involved through organ gratification (sexual pleasure occurring through stimulation of the anal region), and aggression being involved through restriction of the time and place allowed for defecation. No longer can the child empty its bowel when and where it pleases without fear of reprisals. Now it is coaxed by the mother to perform at times chosen for her convenience, and scolded if it does not comply either by defecating on other occasions or by failing to deliver when it is called upon to do so.

If the child complies with the parental wish then it can be considered to be clean, reliable, orderly, and submissive. So when these character traits appear in adult personalities they are taken to originate in libidinal fixation through fear instilled by the mother-child relationship during toilet training. Similarly, non-compliance with the demands of toilet training is taken to be the cause of obstinate, disorderly, parsimonious, unreliable, and stingy behaviour in adulthood, again by analogy with the behaviour of the child who does not freely and reliably give forth of its faeces. And again the plausibility of the thesis is undeniable although its veracity will depend on the individual case.

By about three years of age, Freud has the child entering the *phallic stage*, and in this stage childhood sexuality is actually observed, rather than inferred from material gathered during adult analysis, as was the case with the earlier phases. The possible objection that infantile sexuality is not real because the evidence for it may be no more than adult fantasies recounted during psycho-analysis cannot be seriously maintained, for anyone is free to observe the sexual behaviour of children around three years of age.[40]

Three important concepts in psychoanalytic theory originate in this stage: the *Oedipus complex*, *castration anxiety*, and *penis envy*. These concepts all refer to social relationships within the family – between the child and the parents and between child and child. The supposition is that the boy child forms a sexual attachment to his mother and develops ambivalent feelings toward his father whom he loves as a provider but hates as a sexual rival. This dynamic relationship is described as the Oedipus complex because of its affinity to the plot of Sophocles' play. Erich Fromm[41] has interpreted this play as depicting sibling rivalry rather than father-son rivalry, but this has no bearing on the phenomenon Freud described for he took only the name, not the data, from the Oedipus myth.

It is during the resolution of the Oedipus complex that the principal component of the superego is supposed to develop. The boy child cannot overwhelm the father physically but he can identify with him and introject his ego values and ideals, and these lay the foundations for the formation of the boy's superego. Melanie Klein[42] differs from Freud at this point by assuming that the child takes over the parental superego, not ego. Thus she de-emphasizes the objective situational variable, because it is not the manifest personality of the parent that is introjected, but the perception of the parent formed by the child in its first year.

Castration anxiety is self-explanatory, though its reality is not proven. The little boy might fear castration if it is threatened as a punishment for masturbation, for example. And if he sees his penis-less mother or sister his fears may appear to be real – if the little boy is able to make the appropriate intellectual inference. The little girl with no experience of male anatomy would have no cause to feel penis envy. But when she does become aware of her 'missing member', the psychoanalyst assumes that the little girl assumes that she once had a penis but that it was cut off. By this token she feels herself inferior and has no great love for her mother who has shared the same fate, and who may be blamed for her daughter's predicament.

From the phallic stage, Freud claims that the child passes into a latency period. This is the period when overt sexual behaviour is repressed as a result of the child's superego and its encounters with reality. Anthropologists[43] have pointed out that this does not occur in all cultures, which is embarrassing for the claim that the phases of psychosexual development are biologically determined. But there is no doubt that in some cultures the sexuality exhibited by younger children is no longer observable when they become a little older. There is no need to dismiss this observation on the grounds that it may be wrongly explained by Freudian theory, for other explanations are possible. If, for instance, parents who condone, or fail to recognize, sexuality in infants come to punish or condemn it a few years later, the appearance of a latency period would be expected.

Finally at puberty the sexual libido, if there is anything left of it, comes to rest in the genitalia, and normal reproductive sexuality may begin. If, like the salmon returning upstream to spawn, the libido reaches the pool out of which it was born, the cycle can begin all over again. What has arrived is the normal sexually and socially mature adult personality.

Psychoanalysis, science and imagination[44]

Psychoanalysis is a superb 'prehistoric' scientific system of thought. Freud made a number of acute observations about the dynamics of human behaviour and proceeded to mould these observations into a reasonably consistent theoretical network that was often tied to empirical data, except at one point – the unconscious. Freud committed himself to a belief in the unconscious mind once he had satisfied himself on the functional dependency of neurotic symptoms on childhood experiences, and he then proceeded to make *ad hoc* additions to the unconscious whenever he ran into material that could not be explained by the currently existing structure and its functions. A famous example is his *tour de force* in rescuing psychoanalysis when he learned that the stories of childhood seductions told to him by some of his early female patients, stories that had provided some of the original factual supports for psychoanalytic theory, were untrue. Instead of abandoning his theory at this point, Freud strengthened it by substituting wishful fantasies for actual historical events as the determinants of neurosis, and then, of course, added intrapsychic structures to account for the wishes. Now, some claim, the original stories were true after all![45]

Freud did not make a practice of denying or discounting awkward facts of behaviour but simply expanded his theory to incorporate them. In this way, psychoanalysis grew to be able to explain every kind of behaviour imaginable, but it took the form of a literary rather than a scientific endeavour. A characteristic of a scientific theory is that it does not ignore contradictory evidence, and, up to a point, psychoanalysis can be called scientific on this account, but the scientific solution to refractory data is not to proliferate *ad hoc* theoretical concepts to accommodate such information, but to re-examine the concepts it already has. Because he did not proceed in this way, Freud lost for psychoanalysis any scientific prestige that it might originally have possessed.

If supplementary concepts can be added at will, almost any theory can explain anything – *post hoc*. If I believe that objects fall to the earth because spirits do not like them and throw them back, I can maintain my theory in the face of the fact that helium rises if I add the supplementary belief that the spirits like helium. Likewise an explanation of an event is not verified by the fact that it continually recurs. My explanation of why bodies fall is not proven just because the next rock I throw up falls on my head. Similarly the phenomena reported to recur repeatedly from patient to patient in psychoanalytic sessions have no bearing on the truth or falsity of psychoanalytic theory, even if the facts are reliable.[46]

A scientific theory can only be tested by reference to phenomena that do not contribute to the formulation of the theory. It must permit deductions and predictions about events that the theory was not invented to explain, and even then it is only disproofs of hypotheses derived from a theory that are of permanent value, for when a successful deduction from a theory supports the theory it may also be consistent with other theories not yet conceived. It is not possible to disprove psychoanalytic theory because its concepts are designed to account for all imaginable contingencies. By the same token psychoanalytic principles do not permit behaviour to be predicted. The very strength of psychoanalysis as an explanatory panacea is simultaneously its greatest scientific weakness.[47]

But it is not a mortal weakness. Botany cannot explain the sunflowers of van Gogh, nor astronomy the sunset. 'Love is not love/ Which alters when it alteration finds', is not surpassed by the science of sexual attraction. Science is not just objective, non-judgmental, observation (we see sunsets not earthrises), but observations cloaked in cautious metaphor and imagination. Freud's strength is in imagination and metaphor; his weakness is his lack of caution as an experimental scientist. Freud addressed questions addressed in art and literature for centuries, which the scientific psychology of his time ignored. He failed to provide an explanation of behaviour, but it is better to have addressed the questions and lost than not to have addressed them at all. Even so, Freud contributed to the scientific study of memory at least as significantly as Herman Ebbinghaus, the scientific father of the discipline. In this, Freud's dynamic contextual conception of remembering as a personally meaningful network of associations anticipated the schematic theory of remembering put forward by Sir Frederick Bartlett.[48] And contemporary studies of implicit versus explicit memories owe as much to Freud as they do to Ebbinghaus.[49]

Modern psychology, originating as it does in speculative philosophy, is obsessed with itself as an objective science.[50] So too is contemporary psychiatry through its alliance with modern medicine.[51] As psychoanalysis is speculative and subjective, it is alien to both these disciplines. The case with literature is different, for fiction does not oblige objective 'reality' but creates it. Even if psychoanalysis is science fiction, its influence on fiction and literary criticism is undeniable.[52]

There are two ways to train a psychotherapist: one by rules derived from scientific principles; the other by practical experience. Skinner[53] calls these rule-governed and contingency-shaped situations, respectively. The first of these is learning from the experience of others, the second from experience of oneself. In each of these cases, a system of communication (language) is necessary, in the one case to pass on knowledge from teacher to pupil, in the second to self-observe. The creative writer must be skilled in both of these, the science teacher in the first but not necessarily the second, the psychotherapist in the second, but not necessarily the first.

In science, rules are derived from contingency-shaped experiments – the scientist conducts an experiment (contingency-shaped observation), offers an explanation of his discoveries (hypothesis) and then deduces other findings from this hypothesis. These are put to further test (new contingency-shaped observations) where the hypothesis is either rejected or accepted. Freud omitted this final step. He took the first (or claimed that he did), applied his imagination to the second, but almost totally ignored the third. From imagination alone he concocted rules for training analysts to learn. Trainee scientists who learn from rules alone are no less at risk.

2

Rivals to the Personality Model: Jung, Eysenck, Boss

Psychoanalysis is the first iconoclastic contribution to the knowledge of psychological disorders both from the theoretical and the technical points of view. Although not all theories of personality or all techniques of psychotherapy are actual reactions to Freudian psychoanalysis, nevertheless it has provided a background out of which modern alternative psychologies have developed and against which they may be compared. We may, therefore, examine some of these rivals in this light. In every case, the important thing is not how a total system rivals Freud's, but what it adds to Freud's observations on the one hand, or how it supplants his explanations on the other. Only on the second count does the question of rivalry really arise.

Freud developed a programme of functional psychology that can be symbolized as S-O-R, and developed his programme by speculating about each of these variables. Outside psychoanalysis, other psychological systems have contributed theoretical accounts of one or more of these variables. In this and the following chapters I shall examine some non-Freudian developments of the O-variable, the S-variable, and the R-variable in turn.

Analytical psychology

Analytical psychology is the name given by Carl Jung to his theoretical revision of psychoanalysis. Jung broke with Freud by 1913 over a difference in conception of the nature of the unconscious, and it is his elaboration of the structure of the psyche that justifies consideration of analytical psychology as a development of the

O-variable from psychoanalysis. Jung accepted the unconscious for much the same reasons as Freud, but he populated it quite differently.

Body and mind

Jung believed that the unconscious contained not only 'animal drives' but also the highest human potentialities: intelligence, imagination, creativity. Brain-storming, for example, and some of the wilder inventions of children, can be thought of as problem solving derived from unconscious rather than conscious mental activity. In similar vein, Jung rejected the pansexuality of Freudian psychoanalysis, regarding parent-child relationships as rooted in infantile needs for food, warmth and protection, not simply based on rivalries over sex. For Jung, the child's forgetting of its infantile sexuality was the result of immaturity, not repression. In addition, he invested every individual with a collective as well as a personal unconscious.

Along with elaborating the psyche, Jung insisted on its independence from the body. His justification for this was historical and, in the best sense of the term, modest. Freud believed that the components of the mental apparatus would ultimately reveal themselves as physical structures but Jung, like the behaviourists and the existentialists, disputed this, although his reasons were different from theirs.

According to functional behaviourism, mentality is irrelevant to a generic account of behaviour, as also is the reduction of mental phenomena to physical events. Functional behaviourists take behaviour as their subject-matter and look for lawfulness in behaviour as such, not in mediating mental or physical structures. Existentialism takes mentality as its subject-matter and rejects explanations of psychic phenomena in physical terms because precise details of how neural or glandular activities become thoughts or feelings are neither available nor conceivable. Jung's argument is similar to the existentialists' but he also appeals to history. He speculates that primitive man, taking the facts as they must have appeared before him, believed in the existence of a psyche independent of a body or of consciousness.

To primitive man the psyche is not, as it is to us, the epitome of all that is subjective and subject to the will; on the contrary, it is something objective, contained in itself, and living its own life.[1]

Primitive man is not necessarily right, but neither is modern man. Modern man, impressed by the successes of material science, has tried to deny the independent reality of non-material phenomena (with less confidence now, perhaps, than in the Victorian era) but, says Jung,

To postulate mind is no more fantastic than to postulate matter. Since we have literally no idea of the way in which what is psyche can arise from physical elements, and yet cannot deny the reality of psychic events, we are free to frame our assumptions the other way about for once, and to hold that the psyche arises from a spiritual principle which is as inaccessible to our understanding as matter.[2]

Every age and culture has its outlook on the world, its predominant philosophy, and no proof can be given of the ultimate truth or falsity of any one. An age, or an individual, builds a world on *assumptions*, and Jung prefers the assumptions of primitive man to those of the modern mechanical-material age. It is in this sense that I have called him historical and modest; historical because he realizes that the modern scientific material approach to psychology is not the only approach; modest because he recognizes that *any* approach rests finally on assumption, not on fact. The existentialists have also emphasized that science has many unproven, hidden assumptions at its base, but they have not been as explicit as Jung in recognizing the assumptive nature of their own philosophy of humanity. Jung's doubt, however, soon turned into certainty. 'I know,' he answered when asked if he believed in the existence of God.

The structure of the psyche

The independent psyche that Jung envisaged consists of three primary systems – *persona*, *personal unconscious* and *collective unconscious* – involving balancing tensions both within each system and between them. The persona is the conscious side of the personality, that part of the psyche that shows to the outside world.

But the person is not inwardly what he or she seems to be out-wardly. The persona is like a mask behind which the individual hides by playing social roles. In other terms, it is the individual's behaviour as it has adapted to his or her society. But according to Jung, this is not the real self. The real self involves, among other things, a balance between the persona and its shadow. The *shadow* is the unconscious part of the persona repressed into the personal unconscious, although it also includes elements in the collective unconscious.

Important constituents of the personal unconscious are *com-plexes*. These are conglomerations of associated ideas and affects attached to some person or object. They serve to unify the whole range of behaviour but they are not themselves under conscious control. Jung refers to them as 'autonomous'. That is to say, com-plexes may initiate behaviour without permission of the conscious mind – as in responses to lie detection and word association tests[3] – and they may resist and interfere with the expression of conscious desires. Complexes are weaknesses resulting from unresolved con-flicts and are always liable to expose themselves either as private memories of repressed past events or as public behavioural mani-festations.

Much has been made of Jung's conception of the collective uncon-scious, but it is really only his way of referring to the human-ness of women and men. Be they neurotic or psychotic, sick or well, wise or foolish, humans are first and foremost humans, and it is the collective unconscious that is supposed to carry this heritage of human-ness in the form of *archetypal images*. The archetypes of the collective unconscious are responsible for the way that humans experience the world; they resemble templates from which each individual constructs the universe in common with other people. To change the metaphor, archetypes are the avenues through which people reach out of themselves into the world. How, for example, does man come to know woman, or woman man? Partly, Jung says, from personal experience, not just personal experience impressed upon a *tabula rasa* but experience modulated by the unconscious archetype each sex has of the other. Each man, Jung supposes, possesses an unconscious feminine archetype – his *anima* – and each woman has an unconscious masculine archetype – her *animus*, and when one sex judges a member of the other, the judgment is made not from the qualities of that individual in *vacuo*, but in comparison with the archetypal image of the judge.[4] The archetype relating a person to his or her own sex is the *hero* for the male and the *hetaira* for the female.

The question that Jung is raising is how one comes to know something that is outside oneself. A male may know another male through the common maleness of each, expressed in the archetypal hero; equally the device that enables man to know woman is the femaleness within himself – his anima. This is what provides the link from man to woman, just as the animus is the woman's link with man and the hetaira is one woman's link with another. Other psychologists might refer more prosaically to sexual stereotypes.

Archetypes may be thought to have evolved in humans more or less as they evolved physically. We are accustomed to thinking of evolution only in physical terms, but as the human brain developed it is reasonable to suppose that the human conception of the world changed with it: the evolution of mentality parallels the evolution of anatomy. Throughout the centuries these conceptions have come to take a common form and their 'anatomy' is the archetypal structure of the collective unconscious. To Jung, mind is as real as matter, and as the anatomical structure of ancient man is, so to speak, contained in the bones of his descendants, so the ways in which they perceived the world are contained in our minds today. These contents are the archetypes of the collective unconscious. So archetypes are recognizable by their historical continuity and tenacity, and Jung has analysed myths and dreams, as well as the practices of primitive people, to substantiate his belief in the collective unconscious and its population of archetypes.

Types of personality

The personal and collective unconscious come into contact with the world through the conscious aspect of the psyche. Jung has conceived of several personality types, or rather prototypes, that derive from *attitudes* and *functions* of the conscious mind. The attitudes are the familiar introverted and extraverted outlooks, which refer to inward-turning and outgoing relationships between individuals and the objective world, relationships that are characterized by doubt and withdrawal in the one case, and immediate, confident acceptance in the other.

In general, the introverted attitude is exemplified by reflection rather than by action, by solitude rather than by social engagement, by inward rather than by outward cathexis of the libido. The extraverted attitude is the opposite. When individuals exhibit these attitudes habitually, Jung calls them introverted and extraverted *types*. These attitudes he takes to encompass the whole of a person's existence:

> Introversion or extraversion, as a typical attitude means an essential bias which conditions the whole psychic process, establishes the habitual reactions, and thus determines not only the style of behaviour, but also the nature of subjective experience. And not only so, but it also denotes the kind of compensatory activity of the unconscious which we may expect to find.[5]

It would seem from this passage and others of Jung's writings that he believes the attitudes to be determinants of behaviour, that the style of behaviour is *determined* by introverted or extraverted attitudes.

It is possible to observe in some people the kind of unity of behaviour to which Jung refers, and to describe it in his terms, but it does not follow that the descriptive label is also a causal mechanism. Jung's apparent acceptance of classifications as explanation implies an Aristotelian conception of psychological science as Lewin[6] has described it, in contrast to the functional, Galileian approach.

The attitudes described above are not sufficient to account for all varieties of psychological types and, according to Jung, introverted and extraverted attitudes are tempered by psychic functions. These functions are *thinking*, *feeling*, *sensing* and *intuiting*, of which the first two are described as rational and the last two as non-rational. By rational, Jung means judgmental, the addition of meaning to immediate non-reflexive experience.

The thinking function is the normal mode of logical, rational thinking, but it is not the only way in which the mind works. It can sense as well as think. The sensing function is the functioning of the mind at a purely sensory level: 'I feel warm.' It is non-rational because nothing more than the pure sensory experience of warmth is denoted. The rational counterpart of the sensing function is the function called feeling: 'I feel happy.' The feeling function is emotionally toned experience that includes an evaluation of the sensation. It goes beyond the mere statement of the sensory experience.

There is another sense of feeling – the intuitive feeling that the weather will change, to use Jung's example. This is not the affective feeling of the feeling function nor is it the sensory feeling of the sensing function. It does not involve conscious sensory experience through the sense organs; it is the unconscious aspect of sensing, the imaginative elaboration of unspecifiable sources, and it is this that Jung means by the intuiting function. It is non-rational in the same way as sensing is non-rational. It differs from the thinking function in the sense of when an individual remarks 'Something tells me that you are wrong. I feel you are mistaken,' instead of saying, 'You are wrong because ...'. The mind that uses the rational function of thinking constructs a world of logic, a world of conscious reasons; the one that functions by intuiting acts on hunches.

Jung compares the four psychic functions to the four points of the compass: 'they are just as arbitrary and just as indispensable.' It is possible to shift the cardinal compass points to an infinite number of positions without losing the latitudinal and longitudinal exactitude in locating a particular geographical point; they provide sufficient information for a complete description no matter what their absolute orientation may be. Similarly, Jung would claim, the psychic functions provide a complete framework for a description of mentality:

> Sensing establishes what is actually given, thinking enables us to recognize its meaning, feeling tells us its value, and finally intuition points to the possibilities of the whence and whither that lie within the immediate facts.[7]

Through the functions, Jung dimensionalized psychic processes after the manner of the structural mental philosophers who preceded him and the factor analysts who were his contemporaries. And he knew, as the statistical psychologists came to know, that one set of dimensions can easily, and arbitrarily, be transformed into another.

Every individual is said to have a *superior function* which is that person's normal mode of psychic functioning, and an *inferior function* that is repressed into the unconscious and appears only in dreams, free association and the like. The remaining functions are called *auxiliary functions* and come into operation whenever the superior or inferior function is thwarted. The combinations of habitual attitudes and superior functions yield eight possible personality prototypes, which are summarized in Table 2.1.

The total psyche, then, in Jung's view, is composed of conscious, personal unconscious and collective unconscious elements, all of which exist as an interacting set of forces balanced between and within the different systems. The self is, as it were, the centre of gravity of these forces, the balance of conscious against unconscious, persona against shadow, introversion against extraversion, rational function against non-rational function, and so on.

Jung thought that each conscious facet of personality was offset by its opposite in the unconscious, and that the fully developed personality, the personality that has reached the final stage of *individuation*, was the one in which no part of the psyche has come to outweigh another. In such a personality, thinking is not developed at the expense of feeling, sensing at the expense of intuiting, or consciousness at the expense of the unconscious. To Jung, the unconscious is not a bad thing at all; in fact it is a very necessary part of the full flower of the human personality.

The temporal dimension of the psyche

To the structure of the psyche that has already been described, Jung added another dimension – time. He compared the passage of a person through life to the rising and setting of the sun. In the morning the sun rises and as it rises its rays light up more and more of the earth. In the evening as it descends to the horizon its influence declines. The morning of life contains the stages of childhood and youth, the afternoon and evening, those of middle and old age.[8]

The passage from childhood to youth Jung characterized as the declining dominance of the unconscious in favour of the conscious

Table 2.1. Jung's eight personality prototypes[*]

Superior function	Introverted attitude	Extraverted attitude
Sensing	Emphasis on subjective experiences; concerned with private pleasure, moody and withdrawn.	Emphasis on external world. Takes everything as it comes. Irrational in the sense of no judgement or selection of kind of pleasure.
Thinking	Interested in ideas; facts only important for theory, not for their own sake.	Down-to-earth, interested in facts, not theories. Does not digest information but orders it arbitrarily. More concerned with 'statistics' than with individuals.
Feeling	Emphasis on subjective experiences with some seen as more valuable than others.	Interested in experiences of others, with selection of important from trivial. Principles less important than people's feelings. Right is what people like, not what is best for them.
Intuiting	Mystic, dreamer, crank. Creative artist who expresses subjective feelings. Possibility of revelations and of schizophrenia.	Dislike of established order. Restless and dissatisfied. Ruthless; justifies means by ends. Manic-depressive in extreme cases.

[*] In 'The Waves', Virginia Woolf describes six characters who fit these prototypes, but her descriptions are more dynamic than Jung's. At college, for instance, the student, Bernard, asks himself 'What am I?' and answers 'I am not one and simple, but complex and many.' He goes on, 'Bernard, in public, bubbles; in private, is secretive.'

mind, a change occasioned by the presentation of problems that cannot be solved in unconscious, instinctive ways. Consciousness, in fact, is the solution of problems, the overcoming of obstacles that could not be mastered by purely natural instinctual acts. The dominance of consciousness, Jung claims, continues through the stages of youth and middle age, but by old age, he says, individuals live by their unconscious once again, by turning their glance backwards to the past, not forward to the problems of the future.

It is on account of this temporal dimension of psychic life that Jung differs from Freud and Adler in his conception and treatment of neurosis. To Jung, the neurosis of youth is the unwillingness to enter the future, the hesitation to transfer the control of behaviour from unconscious to conscious forces. These youthful neuroses, he allows, are amenable to cure according to the methods and theories of Adler and Freud. But the neuroses of later life, he claims, are different. The older person's neurosis is a clinging to the past, a dealing with the present according to the consciousness of the past; and it is with cases of this kind that Jung finds that Freudian and Adlerian therapies fail.

Jungian therapy differs from Freudian, in particular, in the matter of the personal relationship between patient and therapist, Jung preferring a more warm, positive attitude to the patient over the cold neutrality employed by the Freudians. This is a move towards interpersonal therapy that others have advocated on theoretical grounds, but Jungian theory has remained entirely intrapsychic. Jung adopted the conventional standpoint that outward appearances are signs of inner dynamics, and that from public behaviour the inner world of the psyche can be inferred. Behind Jung's psychology lies the assumption that the inner world contains the nucleus of the outer world and that when the inner world is understood comprehension of the outer world is automatically achieved.

It is curious that Jung never came to take behaviour seriously in its own right, for he dealt with behaviour, verbal behaviour, all his life. He, like Freud, drew attention to qualities of verbal behaviour that had gone unnoticed before him. He did not dismiss discrepancies between events and verbal accounts of these events as mistakes, but took what people said to be true – true insofar as they revealed the workings of a deeper, hidden psychic structure not amenable to investigation by normal physical means.

Other psychologists have reacted to the unreliability of verbal reports in quite another way. They have dismissed such reports altogether as psychological data and relied instead upon objective psychological tests. They have discovered a modicum of order in people's behaviour from test to test, and by statistical manipulations known as factor analysis have inferred the existence of factors of the mind. Like Jung, factor analysts have tried to reduce the chaos of the psychological world to order but they have relied upon different data and methods: objective instead of introspective, statistical instead of individual. Factor analysts have constructed a picture of personality but it is a different picture from that proposed by Jung and other dynamic psychologists.

Factor analysis

Freud's psychoanalytic system originated in the treatment of a young hysteric woman by Breuer in Vienna; Jung began his career as an alienist in a Swiss asylum for older schizophrenics. Both were medically trained clinicians whose theories derived from clinical pictures of individual patients, and at one time they were friends. H.J. Eysenck is an academically trained psychologist whose theories of personality structure and dynamics started from the responses of soldiers with war neurosis to psychiatric interviews, laboratory tests and questionnaires. Eysenck's theories are based on statistical and experimental evidence; they are the product of imagination, he says[9] but imagination rooted in objective data collected from large normal and neurotic populations, not in personal interactions with mentally sick individuals, as in the cases of Freud and Jung. Nevertheless, Eysenck took as a starting point of his investigations a point of difference between these two men, the question whether neurosis is a matter of exaggerated introversion, as Freud believed, or whether, as Jung thought, introversion-extraversion and neurosis are independent personality dimensions. He concluded in favour of Jung and has been a consistent critic of the 'Freudian Empire' ever since.[10]

The classification of instincts

Factor analysis is a class of statistical methods applicable to problems of classification. It has been employed in psychology for the purpose of discovering the simplest mental structure that can account for the complexity of human personality and abilities. The procedure was originally designed by C.S. Spearman of London University to study the nature of intelligence, and was extended to the elucidation of dimensions of personality by several other psychologists at that University, principally R.B. Cattell and H.J. Eysenck.

At the same time as Freud was developing psychoanalysis and Watson was establishing behaviourism, a school of psychology led by William McDougall was enjoying immense popularity. Very little is heard of McDougall nowadays, but the essence of his system is contained in the factor analytic work of Cattell. McDougall constructed a system of psychology that he called *hormic*. He objected to the teleological implications of *hedonic* psychology based on the assumption that living organisms strive to obtain pleasure and avoid pain, and argued that behaviour is driven by psychological forces rather than pulled by them. In this he agreed with Freud. And, also like Freud, he regarded these forces as instincts. But he was more rigorous than Freud in defining an instinct, which he called

> an inherited or innate psycho-physical disposition which determines its possessor to pay attention to objects of a certain class, to experience an emotional excitement of a particular quality upon perceiving such an object, and to act in regard to it in a particular manner.[11]

The particular style of this definition follows a classical division of mental phenomena into three parts, knowing, feeling and acting, which McDougall incorporated into a single function of instinct. The instinct determined what was perceived in the environment, what was felt about it, and what was done about it. Pleasure and pain were thus the result of the action, not the objective of the action.

This was a *tour de force* as impressive as Freud's, but it too was a piece of legislation rather than a scientific discovery. No satisfactory explanation of how instincts did all the things they were supposed to do was ever given, or even seriously attempted, but the demise of McDougall's system was occasioned not by this but by the impossibility of deciding exactly how many instincts there are. McDougall himself offered anything from half a dozen to a dozen and a half, and altogether numerous instincts were postulated by one ambitious psychologist or another. There are, however, no criteria for deciding whether or not an instinct exists other than the behaviour it is supposed to explain. Every observation of the behaviour of organisms that could not be attributed to an instinct already known was the occasion for another to be invented. There was, apparently, no limit to the instinct list. Freud put an end to this.

The problem, of course, is one of the classification of behaviour. A statistical solution to this problem was offered by Spearman in the course of his investigations into the nature of human intelligence. He showed that by making some simple statistical assumptions he could account for the patterns of intercorrelations (see below) of scores that children obtained in a variety of intellectual tasks on the basis of a general factor common to all the tasks and a set of factors each one specific to each of the tasks. As it happened, Spearman's work did not go unchallenged and he did not settle the question of what is intelligence once and for all, but his methods were taken up in London by Cattell and Eysenck to elucidate the structure of personality.[12]

The structure of personality

To J.B. Watson, the founder of behaviourism, personality is but the end product of our habit systems, but others, such as Gordon Allport and Jung, have described personality in terms of personality traits and personality types. Eysenck united these ways of describing personality into a hierarchical system beginning with individual acts and ending with personality types. The act is the lowest rung in the system, and some acts are more typical of an individual than are others. These typical acts are what we call habits, and they tend to persist over time. This is Watson's level of description; it specifies what can be called longitudinal consistency of personality.

Without habits, we could not rely on anything about an individual's behaviour over time, and a notion of personality could not exist. But with a habit system alone a description of personality would be formidable. The task is easier if habits themselves form into groups, such as fun-loving, shy, irritable and honest. This is the level of personality traits; it is a transverse organization of habits. And then traits may be transversely organized into types, such as the familiar outgoing extraverts and reserved introverts. Eysenck follows Jung in advocating these as basic human personality types. These types are constellations of traits that lie along a personality dimension from one extreme of extraversion, through ambiversion to introversion at the other. The types are not discrete categories of persons, but values along a dimension of personality. Figure 2.1 is a pictorial representation of Eysenck's hierarchical system.

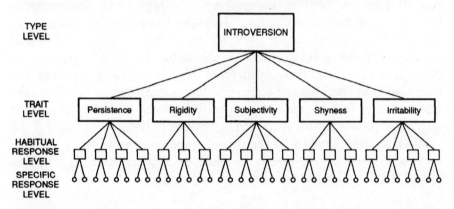

Figure 2.1. Representation of Eysenck's view of the organization of personality. The lowest level refers to specific acts, such as sticking to a difficult task. The next level of organization is the habitual repetition of such acts, and the level above that refers to the fact that some habits, such as rigidity and persistence, are positively correlated. Type level, the highest, depicts the clustering of individual traits. A similar organization exists for the extraverted type. For a more complete picture see H.J. Eysenck, *The Structure of Human Personality*, London: Methuen, 1953. Reproduced with permission.

It is plain from the figure that the way in which the types are arrived at does not permit them to be used causally. Persons who sit shyly in a corner in the midst of a party are called introverted because they exhibit this and correlated behaviour that defines the type. We cannot then say that such people behave as they do because they are introverted; they are called introverted because of their typical habits. The reason for the introverted behaviour cannot be found in the habits themselves. It must be sought elsewhere, and Eysenck's theories in this connection are considered below.

The neurotic personality

A questionnaire given to groups of hospitalized soldiers at the end of World War I uncovered a number of differences between a group diagnosed as neurotic and a normal group with physical wounds alone. Among these differences, more soldiers in the neurotic than in the normal group claimed to suffer from heart palpitations, to worry over humiliation, and to suffer from nervousness and easily hurt feelings. They also had inferiority feelings and worried about possible misfortunes.

Some of the normal soldiers also endorsed these attributes, but they were relatively few. Among the neurotics, half or more admitted to at least one of these characteristics in themselves. With another neurotic group, emotional instability, apprehensiveness, childhood shyness, and marital and sexual difficulties were rated by psychiatrists more frequently than in a normal group of control subjects.

On Eysenck's laboratory tests, neurotic soldiers proved inferior to non-neurotics in body sway suggestibility, static ataxia, ability to follow a moving light with a pointer, dark vision, visual acuity and accommodation. Thus, so far as the neurotic personality in general is concerned, without regard to any particular symptomatology the neurotic admits to feelings of inferiority, nervousness and worrying, is rated by psychiatrists as emotionally and sexually unstable, and is deficient in bodily motor control and certain visual processes.

Differential symptomatology

The neurotic personality as such does not differentiate the classical subtypes of hysteria and anxiety neurosis (which Eysenck calls dysthymia). They may be entirely different clinical sub-categories or one may be simply a more severe neurosis than the other. The problem may be resolved by factor analysis.

Factor analysis is a mathematical system of classification. It is based on the assumption that the degree of correlation (from zero to unity) between two sets of events is an index of commonality of origin of the two events. Consider the following: A group of students is given four examinations, one each of arithmetic (A), grammar (G), history (H) and literature (L). Each student obtains a mark on each test and the marks are correlated to see if students who do well on one test also do well on the other. Thus, if those who do well on tests of proficiency in grammar also do well on tests of knowledge of literature, the correlation of the two sets of scores will approach 1.0; and if those who score highly on arithmetic also do well on history tests, those sets of scores will also correlate 1.0. But if arithmetic and history marks are unrelated to those of grammar and literature then the correlations between these sets of marks will be zero. The correlations between all of the pairs can be expressed as a matrix in which the pattern of relationships between the test results can be detected:

Exam	A	H	L	G
A	–	1.0	0.0	0.0
H	1.0	–	0.0	0.0
L	0.0	0.0	–	1.0
G	0.0	0.0	1.0	–

This example is artificial and elementary, and the classification of the four examinations into two pairs is visually obvious. With many sets of real data that correlate imperfectly, however, statistical procedures are necessary to uncover any pattern that may exist between them. (The pattern so found will be unique for a particular input of items, but alternative factorial interpretations of the pattern are not excluded by the computational procedure.)

Such a procedure applied to psychiatric ratings of 700 neurotic soldiers on 39 characteristics such as breadth of interests, abnormality in parents, obsessional, hysterical attitude, anxiety, apathy, depression, sex anomalies and hypochondriasis yielded a general factor common to all the soldiers and a bipolar factor that divided them into two groups. The general factor, labelled 'Neuroticism' by Eysenck, included such items as badly organized personality, dependence, hypochondriasis, dyspepsia and schizoid personality. Two sub-groups, typified by sex anomalies, hysterical conversion, narrow interests, poor work record and little energy, on the one

hand, and anxiety, depression, irritability, obsessional and apa-
thetic, on the other, identified the bipolar factor. These sub-groups
Eysenck labelled 'Hysteria' and 'Dysthymia'. Subsequently he generalized this analysis from the abnormal to the normal personality
and identified two principal dimensions of personality: stability-
instability, following Freud, and extraversion-introversion, following Jung. On these dimensions, unstable extraverts and unstable
introverts are, respectively, the classical hysterical and anxiety states.

Conditioning and personality

Fundamentally Freud's theory of neurosis is a learning theory. For
him, neurotic symptoms are reactions to life experiences, and these
reactions serve to remove the individual from unpleasant personal
and social circumstances. The unpleasantness is removed, according to Freud, by repression into the unconscious, and the
unconscious proceeds to take control of behaviour. Part of this
control is vested in the superego, making the neurotic overstrained
in his or her social behaviour, or, in general, oversocialized. Although this may be a plausible account of the dysthymic
personality, it ignores the undersocialized behaviour of the hysteric, as described above. It also ignores the psychology of learning.
Freud can hardly be blamed for this, because this field of psychology
was underdeveloped in his time, although Pavlov's research on
conditioning was well developed before Freud died.

Learning theory was taken up and applied to the theory and
treatment of neurosis by Joseph Wolpe and others, but Eysenck has
been one of its most consistent protagonists, especially from the
standpoint of conditioning according to Pavlov. Like Freud's,
Eysenck's theory changed in the face of evidence, and three
Eysenckian conditioning theories of neurosis can be identified, two
based on properties of the nervous system and one on the nature of
conditioning.

The first theory

Eysenck's first theory of the dynamics of anxiety and hysteria
derived from the concepts of neural excitation and inhibition elaborated by the American learning theorist, Clark Hull, from earlier

work of Pavlov (see Chapter 4). Hull calls the tendency to make a certain act its *excitatory potential* (sEr), which is the product of the *habit strength* (sHr) of that act and the motivation, or *drive* (D) to perform it. Drive, in Hull's system, is similar to motivation in Freud's insofar as both are energized by deprivation, but in Hull's case, drive reduction strengthens a motor habit rather than an unconscious population. Hull expressed the relationship between habit strength, drive strength and the potential for action in the form

$$sEr = sHr \times D$$

From this formulation Hull subtracted inhibitory potential composed of reactive inhibition, or fatigue (Ir), and conditioned inhibition (sIr), a learned habit of resting when fatigued. As inhibition mounts so it subtracts from sEr so that the resultant tendency to react can be expressed by

$$sEr = (sHr \times D) - (sIr + Ir)$$

Eysenck employed the concept of inhibition to differentiate hysterics from dysthymics. He began, as did Freud, in taking inappropriate socialization as the hallmark of neuroticism, and accounted for the difference between the undersocialized hysteric and the oversocialized dysthymic in terms of the reactivity of their nervous systems in the Hullian sense. Thus he argued that in hysterics (or extraverts in general), inhibitory potential (which opposes the learning of social habits) develops more quickly, becomes stronger and decays more slowly than in introverts.

After a good beginning in which some predictions from the theory were upheld, such as one that hysterics should condition more slowly than dysthymics in the laboratory, Eysenck abandoned this theory. It turned out to be unsatisfactory because individual differences in speed of conditioning depend on the type of conditioned response regardless of extraversion-introversion, and because the Hullian foundation on which the theory was built was flawed.

The second theory

One change from the first to the second theory of hysteria and dysthymia is from speed of conditioning to a cortical arousal theory of extraversion-introversion. The second theory calls on individual differences in levels of arousal of the ascending reticular activating system (ARAS) to account for extraverted and introverted behaviours.

The ARAS is part of the central nervous system that responds non-specifically to sensory stimulation. All specific sensory stimuli, lights and sounds, for instance, arouse the organism by stimulating the ARAS at the same time as they elicit specific neural responses in their respective cortical locations. Thus the senses serve to activate as well as to inform, and it is the innate level of arousal of an individual that, Eysenck believes, determines the degree to which a person behaves in an extraverted manner. The theory postulates that extraverts have low innate levels of arousal and so engage in vigorous behaviours that raise arousal levels; introverts, on the other hand, are more highly aroused to begin with, so they avoid the excitable situations that extraverts enjoy.

Although it appeals to physiological rather than to mental substrates, and is laboratory rather than clinically based, this inward-outward balance of excitability (underaroused inwardly, extraverted outwardly; overaroused inwardly, introverted outwardly) is remarkably similar to Jung's opposition of unconscious with conscious attitudes. Jung's postulation of a collective human unconscious also corresponds to an appeal by Eysenck to historical continuity as support for his four-fold categorization of personality. In this, Eysenck relates his structural theory of personality to the classical humoric theory of temperaments depicted in Figure 2.2.

Jung's collective unconscious is also an appeal to continuity of human personality over the ages. In both men, clinician and academician, although they express it differently, there is explicit recognition that human nature cannot have changed throughout recorded time.

A novelty in Eysenck's theoretical development is the introduction of a new terminology in which the subclasses of neurosis are labelled disorders of the first and disorders of the second kind.[13] The new terminology represents a change of emphasis from a structural

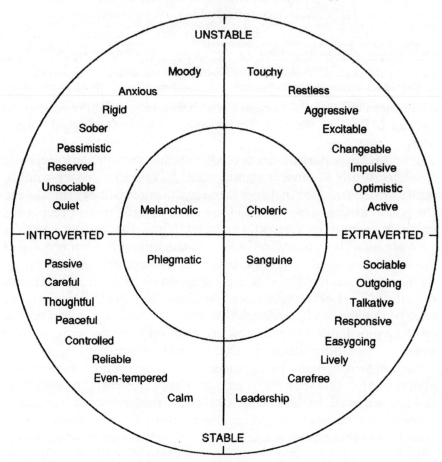

Figure 2.2. In this figure, Eysenck relates his dimensions of personality to the classical humoric theory of temperament. For a fuller account of this relationship, see H.J. & M.W. Eysenck (eds.), *Personality and Individual Differences: A Natural Science Approach*, New York: Plenum Press, 1985. Reproduced with permission.

to a functional account of neurosis and effectively renders the structural dimensions redundant. They were relevant to the genesis of the system in delineating sub-groups of neurosis from a unitary category of neurosis, but they are marginal to the second theory, where the stress is on the genesis of neurotic *behaviour*. Structure now is a physiological substrate, not a direct organization of behaviour.

Disorders of the first and second kinds refer, respectively, to dysthymic and hysteric reactions. The first kind includes obsessive-compulsive behaviour, phobic reactions, anxiety states and psychophysiological disorders; the second kind includes psychopathy, antisocial behaviour, and sexual maladjustment. The two kinds of disorder are differentiated by their provenance: disorders of the first kind are the result of inappropriate conditioning; disorders of the second kind are failures of conditioning. In the first case, inappropriate conditioning would be conditioned fear of an actually harmless object. The acquisition of the fear might be realistic in the first place, but additional acquaintance with the harmless object should, by orthodox conditioning theory, result in fear extinction. With neurotic fear, extinction does not occur, and Eysenck's third theory is directed to this anomaly.

Two possible conditioning failures are proposed in the case of disorders of the second kind. One is direct symptom conditioning, as, for instance, of a fetish; the other is the failure of avoidance learning. According to O.H. Mowrer (and also to Sigmund Freud), the developing individual becomes socialized through punishment of socially unacceptable behaviours. In the normal case, Mowrer argued, whenever such punished behaviours begin to recur they act as conditioned stimuli for incompatible behaviour that serves to avoid the potential punishment.

Eysenck's neurotic disorders of the second kind are not the normal case of learned avoidance behaviour. This kind of neurosis occurs, Eysenck theorizes, because appropriate avoidance behaviour has not become conditioned.

The third theory

In his third theory, Eysenck proposes less a model of neurosis than a theory of conditioning. He reverts to a undimensional account of neurosis, which he defines as follows:

> maladaptive behaviour, accompanied by strong, irrelevant and persistent emotions, occurring in full awareness of the maladaptive and irrational nature of the behaviour in question. Typical instances ... are anxiety reactions, phobias, obsessional-compulsive behaviour, reactive depressions and psychosomatic systems.[14]

Eysenck is explicit about this being a definition of neurosis of the first kind, and is aware that the category of neurosis is no longer a psychiatric diagnostic label everywhere. (It is omitted in favour of specific sub-categories in the third version of the American Statistical and Diagnostic Manual.) This is not a defect of Eysenck's third theory, however, because it is a theory of conditioning based on apparently maladaptive behaviours regardless of their labels. The revision of conditioning theory hinges on the concepts of preparedness and incubation.

Preparedness describes the proposition that organisms are genetically prepared to associate some events more easily than others. Prey that do not flee naturally from predators have little opportunity to learn to do so, and organisms that flee from everything would rapidly die of starvation. Most of the experimental research on learning has been done with arbitrary stimuli and arbitrary responses, but some responses are elicited more easily by some stimuli than by others. Avoidance learning, for instance, is very difficult to teach to a rat if the avoidance response is pressing a bar, but is very easy if the response is running or jumping out of a box. Taste avoidance learning, likewise, is learned with long interstimulus intervals when the taste (Conditioned Stimulus) is paired with nausea (Unconditioned Stimulus), but not when the taste is paired with electric shock. Similarly, higher order appetitive conditioning is stronger when the first and second order conditioned stimuli are in the same sense modality (e.g. light-light) than when the sense modalities are different (e.g. light-tone).

The significance of preparedness for Eysenck's third theory of neurosis is less to do with acquisition than with extinction. In this respect he approvingly quotes Seligman to the effect that human phobias are 'highly prepared ... selective ... and ... resistant to extinction'. Explanation of the persistence, or resistance to extinction, of phobias is a principal objective of the third theory. The explanation is founded on the concept of incubation.

According to this, under some circumstances occurrence of a conditioned stimulus (CS) in the absence of the unconditioned stimulus (US) leads to the strengthening of the conditioned response (CR) instead of to its weakening, as normal conditioning theory requires (see Chapter 4). Such strengthening without reinforcement brings up a fundamental question for the theory of extinction. A possible answer is that humans can imagine phobic stimuli even when they are absent, and respond either by fear or by taking avoiding action in deed or thought (repression). In the first of these alternatives, fear would be strengthened by the presence of the imagined phobic object (reinforcement by respondent conditioning) and in the second case, avoidance would be strengthened (negatively reinforced) by the removal of the object of the phobia (operant conditioning). Eysenck elects not to evoke a psychology of imagination to explain the conditioning anomaly but to revise the theory of extinction.

The essence of the revised theory has elements in common with Eysenck's first theory of neurosis. In that theory, Eysenck adopted Clark Hull's idea that response acquisition also involves response inhibition; in the present theory, his conjecture is that response extinction also involves response excitation. Eysenck says:

> Our argument will be that the presentation of the CS unaccompanied by a UCS always provokes a decrement in CR strength, but that it may also provoke an *increment* in CR strength so that the observed CR is the resultant of two opposing tendencies: *extinction* if the decrementing tendencies are greater [or] ... *incubation* if the incrementing tendencies are greater ...[15]

Put in the form of the Hullian equation given above, this amounts to:

$$sEr = sHd - sHi$$

where the tendency to respond in extinction (sEr) is the algebraic sum of response decrement (sHd) and response increment (sHi). Eysenck specifies parameters under which sHi should be greater than sHd, and thus generate incubation rather than extinction, but confesses that his theory is heuristic rather than definitive.

Daseinsanalysis

Despite its dynamic quality, Freud's personality system is fundamentally reactive – responsive rather than active. Freud's system is also atomistic, as also are those of Eysenck and Jung. Gordon Allport[16] calls such systems Lockean and points to an alternative structuralization in the tradition of Leibnitz. This tradition stresses the active, intentional and holistic nature of personality. Into this tradition fits existential psychiatry.

Existential psychiatry, led by Ludwig Binswanger and Medard Boss in Europe and by Rollo May in the United States, derives its impetus from philosophical existentialism stretching back from Jean Paul Sartre and Martin Heidegger through Edmund Husserl to the Danish philosopher-theologian Soren Kierkegaard. Unlike psychoanalysis, which originated in the psychiatric clinic and then extended its influence into psychology and literature, existentialism came into psychiatry from the outside. Existentialism is not a closed society and represents not a particular packaged philosophy but a general attitude towards human nature that recognizes its dignity, its value and its freedom. The daseinsanalysis of Medard Boss is a particular case of this philosophy applied to psychiatry.[17]

Daseinsanalysis is not an entirely different therapy from psychoanalysis, and Boss has argued that Freudian therapy actually flows more naturally from existential theory than from Freud's own theory of psychoanalysis. Be that as it may, there are fundamental differences between daseinsanalysis and psychoanalysis in theory: psychoanalysis is functional where daseinsanalysis is phenomenological, psychoanalysis is atomistic where daseinsanalysis is holistic, psychoanalysis is dualistic where daseinsanalysis is monistic, psychoanalysis regards the present as the product of the past. The present, to the daseinsanalyst, is real as it is, emergent from the past, but not ruled by it.

Da sein means, literally, *to be there* – to be, so to speak, in one's existence, and is perhaps best expressed by the contemporary slang expression 'getting one's self together'. The extent to which one is together is the phenomenon with which Boss is concerned, and he sees his task as helping his patients to fulfil themselves rather than analysing forces supposedly controlling their actions. By the same token, he sees each human being as a unity. Everything done and felt is an expression of this unity, not the result of interacting personality parts, like id, ego, and superego, persona and shadow, or factors of introversion, intelligence, neuroticism and so on.

To the daseinsanalyst, as to the behaviourist, what one does, one is. A Freudian-like dualism of mind in charge of matter is superfluous and irrelevant to existential analysis. Existentialism is monistic in the sense that it denies the distinction between individuals and their surroundings. One exists in the texture of one's environment, not apart from it or as part of it, but in it and as it – 'man always and from the beginning fulfils his existence *in* and *as* one or the other mode of behaviour in regard to something or somebody.'[18] There is not one *and* other people, one *and* the physical world but one *in* the texture of somebody or something. In the more down to earth language of the behaviourist, behaviour does not exist in a vacuum, it affects, and is affected by, something or somebody. Behaviourism and daseinsanalysis are alike in rejecting the reduction of the data of psychology to the data of physiology, and neither regards the physical world as illusory.

Boss's claim that the world exists only through the human mind does not mean that it exists only in a person's mind. Dasein is, as it were, a torch that illuminates whatever it shines upon, but it does not create it. The goal of daseinsanalysis is to understand behaviour, not to explain it, and the basis of this understanding is the assumption of the fundamental unity of one's being-in-the-world, and this unity, it is said, is exhibited in every facet of a person's existence. Behaviour to Boss is sufficiently explained by reference to the unity of existence:

> If some special thing in the room is of great interest to me at the moment, if it means a great deal to me, I will probably approach it bodily also. For my body is a partial sphere of my existence ... In approaching this thing bodily, I have merely fulfilled by existential closeness to it in regard to the bodily sphere of my existence, *a closeness which already existed.*[19]

Being-in-the-world

Although the existentialist stresses the wholeness, the unity of being 'with it' in all aspects of the world simultaneously, he or she must, like anyone else, make abstractions about the conditions of existence. The existentialist must dimensionalize existence in order to discuss it, and the dimensions employed are time and space. There are four modes of relatedness to the world, or four facets of being in the world, one 'temporal' and three 'spatial'.

Dasein, being there, exists in *time* and in *space*, but the temporality and spatiality are not in the conventional physical dimensions.

The temporal mode

For Boss, time is always the present, but the present includes all that has remained with dasein from its past, and all its aspirations for the future. Time is psychological time: *Every 'now' and every 'then' refers to a man's caring for something, and it lasts as long as this caring-for lasts.*[20] This is how the past is brought psychologically into the present.

Concerning the future, Van den Berg[21] gives an illustration used by Erwin Straus. He refers to the behaviour of a man leaping a ditch, rightly claiming that the behaviour of arriving on the other side is already determined before the leap begins. One is encouraged to 'look before you leap'. One will not, normally, leap out into darkness, and this, it is concluded, makes sense only if the behaviour on arrival is already there from the start. As Van den Berg describes it: 'The present, so we might condense it into a few words, is the going to meet myself as I throw myself as what I have become into the future.'

The general existential emphasis on acceptance of the immediacy of phenomena rather than on reflection about them applies to time and space. In the immediate experience of it, one knows what time is, and knows it by *acquaintance*; but on reflection, on searching for knowledge *about* time one is defeated. St Augustine remarked concerning time: 'When someone asks me what time is, I know, but when I would give an explanation of it ... I do not know.' To this, the existentialists agree. To them, *knowledge about time* is irrelevant to psychology, for one's temporal existence lies in one's *knowledge of acquaintance* with time, and that alone.

The spatial modes

As well as the temporal mode of relatedness to the world, existential analysts stress three 'spatial' modes of relatedness: existence in the actual physical world (*unwelt*), existence in the body (*eigenwelt*), and existence in relationships with other people (*mitwelt*). Boss accuses psychoanalysis of dealing only with the umwelt, the world in which one *adjusts*, or to which one reacts passively. Sullivan, on the other hand, emphasizes mitwelt, the interpersonal relations of individual with individual. To Boss, a person exists in relatedness to the world in all three ways – mitwelt, umwelt and eigenwelt, simultaneously and in unity over time. Without this relatedness one does not exist at all. In all these modes of existence, Van den Berg contrasts the objective with the subjective, the reflective with the pre-reflective, the physical with the existential-psychological world.

Relatedness to the physical world. The objective world is the physical, material world. It is the world that shines in the light of dasein for any particular person but, that world also exists independently of that person, it is the same for everyone. The subjective world of the individual is the *significance* of the object, and the significance is psychological and personal. The objective world may be the *true* world, physically speaking, but it is the subjective world that is the *real* world so far as the individual is concerned. From the objective point of view a person's perception of an event may be mistaken – he or she may hallucinate, for example, or impute sinister motives to his or her neighbours – but subjectively there are no mistakes: 'while telling us what his world looks like, he tells us without prevarication, without any mistake, *how he is himself.*'[22]

There is, for the existentialist, no explaining away a person's misperceptions, no correcting them or accounting for them in a separate set of theoretical terms. What a person sees is isomorphic with that person's personality; one *is* what one sees. If I perceive my world crumbling about me it is *I* who am crumbling and about to fall apart; if I see my world as safe and secure it is I myself who exists in safety and security. The world of a person shines in that person's dasein – there can be no mistake, only illumination.

There is a clear similarity between the existential contention that what one sees, one is, and the Freudian conception of projection, but the two views agree only in that such a phenomenon exists. The existentialist rejects the whole Freudian mental apparatus as superfluous and finds no need for it; neither for an ego to defend itself nor for an id or a superego to be defended against. Nor does the existential analyst see how an 'effect' can be detached from one object and projected out onto another. From the existential point of view, person and world are one, there is no subject-object dichotomy, no projector and projected-onto, only a unity of existence in which everything is consistent – 'what a man is inwardly that he will see outwardly'.

Relatedness to one's body. Malfunction of the body is the proper concern of medical science, but it is not uncommon to find physical failings unaccompanied by structural, somatic defects. Freud (and Breuer) called these conversion hysterias, referring to the conversion of psychological into physical illness, but Van den Berg prefers to conceptualize two different bodies, the one arrived at after reflection, the solely physical structure, and the body of immediate experience. This second 'body' is the phenomenological body that is the 'me' of the child before it learns that its body is not him or her at all but only a vehicle that carries 'me' around. When this phenomenological body fails in one or other of its aspects, it is not for any of the usual physical reasons but through a constriction of existence. The particular symptoms exhibited by this body are the clues to the manner in which this person relates to the world.

The notion that one *has* a body (reflective) and *is* a body (pre-reflective) at one and the same time is rejected by Boss. To him, 'the existential approach maintains that man's somatic aspect is inseparable from his being-in-the world'.[23] In his view, one relates to the world through one's body, and where there is a failure of relatedness it may appear either as conversion hysteria or as organ neurosis (psychosomatic illness). Both these disorders, Boss contends, mean that 'one gives up the freedom to be open to the world in all the ways available' and that they differ in *degree of concealment*, with hysteria more open to the world, more interpersonal, and organic neuroses more inner directed.

Relatedness to others. The third 'spatial' facet of being-in-the-world is one's relatedness to others. The expansion of one into one's being – with oneself, with the world, and with others – follows a course that may or may not be deflected by the circumstances of an individual's upbringing.

Boss does not specify what these circumstances might be, or how existential relatedness comes about, but he cannot avoid the question, because when psychotherapy is required it necessitates therapist and patient joining into a common existence. The therapist who succeeds in this must hold the secret of being. One who can forge a common existence with another must in fact have some idea of how being-in-the-world can come about.

The shift from psychoanalysis to daseinsanalysis is a shift from an intrapsychic to an interpersonal theory of human nature, and from an impersonal to an interpersonal therapeutic technique. The psychoanalyst reacts to the patient, and may be cold and distant; the daseinsanalyst interacts with patients and endeavours to be one with each one of them to the best of his or her ability.

All these 'spatial' modes of relating to the world exist in time. I have already reviewed the existential account of time but there is one further consideration to be made. This pertains to the therapeutic phenomenon of transference. Boss does not contest Freud's observation of transference but he does dispute the interpretation that it represents a repetition of the patient's early life. Transference is not, according to Boss, a representation of the past in the present, but an interaction in the present that is the same as an interaction in the past. What is happening, he says, is that patients behave towards their therapists as they behaved towards their parents, but the therapeutic relationship is a *new* relationship for the patient, and his or her love or hate for the therapist is genuine and real. A patient relates to the therapist in the same way as that patient related to a parent in the past; it is not a transference of the past into the present, but consistency in a mode of relating.

Like the behaviourist, the existentialist discards as superfluous the constructs of psychoanalytic theory in accounting for the continuity of behaviour over time, but the existentialist claims to *understand* the present through its unity with the past, not to *explain* it as a function of the past. Whatever determined behaviour in the past, according to Boss, also determines it now, but how this determining factor operates, existentialism does not say. That is the province of the behaviourist.[24]

Levels of relatedness

Interpersonal relations, according to Weigert,[25] may occur on the level of *Love* or on the level of *Care*. The level of Care is the impersonal level of 'one' – in this world one works, one plays, one eats, etc. – not the personal level of 'I', or 'he' or 'we' or 'John', and so on.

Adjustment is possible on the level of Care; the human attitude to death is an example. Death is an important temporal item in life for it is the great inevitability that pervades every human life. As the future is in the present, so the presentiment of death is a permanent feature of existence, and one can continue in the face of this inevitability because, it is said, one adjusts to it impersonally – one dies, or everyone dies, not I shall die.

Relatedness to the world may occur entirely and only at the level of Care. In an existence of this sort, security may be obtained by *using* other people, by relating to them for selfish gain, by role playing, by modifying one's demeanour to meet the exigencies of the hour. At this level, behaviour is opportunistic, not genuine, spontaneous or sincere.

A true, creative, independent security is attainable only at the existential level of Love, where interrelations are genuine, personal, spontaneous, and non-reflective. The task of the psychotherapist is to transport his or her patient from a level of Care to the level of Love, and to do this, the therapist must meet the patient in the plane of Love, or, as Carl Rogers says, grant him or her unconditional positive regard. This is not the attitude of the psychoanalyst:

> In existentialist terms, psychoanalysis gives an opportunity to experience the duality of experience not as Love, since doctor and patient are bound to existence as Care: the patient using the doctor, the doctor taking care of the patient ...[26]

But, if one is to benefit from therapy, one must not use or be used by the doctor. The patient must actualize his or her own existence and the therapist can assist by joining him or her on the plane of Love. Not safe in Care but secure in Love. These different levels of relatedness are outside the provinces of clinical psychoanalysis and experimental psychology.

3

Rivals to the Personality Paradigm: Adler, Sullivan

Although I have described the theory of psychosexual development as a development of the S-variable within psychoanalysis, this is only partly true. While the theory does draw attention to certain critical environmental factors that may influence the psychic development of children, Freud's emphasis, in contrast to that of Karl Abraham, was on the ways in which training practices could interfere with the normal biological growth of psychic forces, not with the shaping of these forces by situational circumstances. Even though Freud's first theory of neurosis did stress historical incidents in a patient's life as responsible for neurotic, particularly hysteric, symptoms, he abandoned this approach, claiming that tales of infantile sexual assault that he had heard from his earliest patients were fantasies rather than accounts of actual events.[1]

Although this might have caused Freud to reject his theory of the sexual aetiology of neurosis, it actually strengthened his belief in the pervasiveness of sexuality, and altered the course of psychoanalytic theory from one concerned with the effects of sexual incidents on personality to one concerned with the intrapsychic development of sexuality itself. That is, psychoanalysis focused on the biological development of sexual libido within itself rather than on interpersonal or situational events of a sexual nature. Hence the theory of psychosexual development is a theory about the natural, normal biological unfolding of the libido, and it is in this sense that the situational events to which Freud and other psychoanalysts have referred must be regarded as hurdles that the developing libido must overcome, and not as factors directly responsible for determining later behaviour.

Objections to Freud's exclusive concentration on biological determination of behaviour stem from several sources, one of the best known being the neo-Freudian school of psychoanalysts led by Karen Horney, Erich Fromm and Harry Stack Sullivan. The ideological linkages between these analysts are relatively loose, but all agree in stressing the sociological nature of mankind at the expense of its biological, instinctual side. Horney, in particular, has drawn attention to a number of possible human social needs, but in so doing she diverted attention from classes of behaviour exhibited in social surroundings to a set of inner, O-variable, energizing needs.

The most drastic innovations within neo-Freudianism were made by Sullivan, himself influenced by Adolf Meyer and William Alanson White, as well as by Freud. But before undertaking a detailed consideration of Sullivan's contribution to psychological theory, we should examine the views of an earlier critic of orthodox psychoanalysis, Alfred Adler.

Individual psychology

Adler was one of the first to join Freud's psychoanalytic circle, being a founder member of the Psychological Wednesday Society, formed in 1902. He resigned from the society in 1911, three years after it had blossomed into the Vienna Psychoanalytical Society, and later founded his own school of psychology which he named *Individual psychology*. Adler differed from Freud in adopting a sociological, interpersonal, situational-variable approach to psychology, in contrast to the orthodox biological, intraphysic, organism-variable position. It is amusing to note that Adler's choice of sociological rather than biological factors as the principal determinants of human behaviour is frequently explained by his opponents as being the result of his socialistic tendencies, which can be explained by the social and family conditions in which he grew up! Ernest Jones for instance, remarks: 'It is not irrelevant to recall that most of Adler's followers were, like himself, ardent Socialists ... This consideration makes it more intelligible that Adler should concentrate on the sociological aspects of consciousness rather than on the repressed unconscious.'[2] A rather remarkable admission for an orthodox, biologically oriented opponent of Adler's point of view.

Even more remarkable is Freud's quip on learning just before

World War I that Adler had been invited to lecture in the United States – 'Presumably the object is to save the world from sexuality and base it on aggression'[3] – for Freud came to adjust psychoanalysis in just this direction soon after the war was over.

Social and personal interest

Adler's difference with Freud is more than a mere substitution of aggression for sexuality. While it is true that Adlerians believe that there is a basic human need for superiority, this need is not a selfish desire to dominate, as is the case with the Freudian id, but a striving to overcome an initial inferiority – the inferiority and weakness of the child in a world of adults. It is a need to *cope* with society, not to subjugate it, at least in its normal expression.

For survival, coping is less of a need than a necessity. The infant begins its life at the mercy of its physical and social environment and must necessarily overcome this initial liability to continue to exist. Whether or not the resulting coping behaviour is normal or competitive and self-centered, which Adler regards as abnormal, is said to depend upon the concurrent development of *social interest*, which itself results from the infant's interpersonal relations within the family, particularly with the mother for she is the principal source of social contact for the child in its early years.

According to Adler, the child is innately capable of love and affection, and if its love is properly reciprocated by the mother, the child's behaviour 'blossoms forth' and extends to interaction between the individual and other members of its community. When social interest is weak as a result of neglect or denigration of the child by the mother then the striving for superiority takes on an aggressive flavour of domination and self-interest. Adler's conception of human nature as inherently good and sociable contrasts starkly with the Freudian standpoint that man is basically selfish and bad. In Adler's case the individual and his or her community are for each other; they fall into disharmony only if the community fails the individual and stunts his or her social interest. In Freud's case, the aim of society is to *tame* the individual, who is condemned to live out his or her life on a battleground where the forces of libido battle with the introjected values of the community for control of the individual's behaviour.

Unlike psychoanalysts and factor analysts, Adler does not fractionate personality into parts, such as ego, id and superego, or into various traits, but considers it as a single unified whole exemplified by the style of life. Behaviour is not the result of interacting psychic forces, nor the product of a number of separate personality traits, but a unique and unitary whole. It is not a whole composed of parts but an organization of parts subservient to the whole. 'The whole commands the parts', meaning that no matter which of the various aspects of a personality may be 'visible' at any one time they are all directed by a single overriding goal established and maintained by a unique style of life. So far as personality is concerned, Adlerian psychology is far more interested in the uniqueness of the individual than in commonalities between one individual and another. Individual psychology is idiographic rather than nomothetic, morphological rather than dimensional in its emphasis, in Gordon Allport's terms.[4]

Real and fictional goals

The psychological world with which a person interacts is not the objective world of physics but the subjective, phenomenological world, the world as he or she perceives it. The style of life is governed by what Adler calls fictive, or *fictional* goals. These are not necessarily wrong or misguided, but they are personal. Stimulation from the outside world is not passively received but actively created into perceptions that are understandable in terms of a life style. These private, subjective perceptions and interpretations are a result of the outcomes of interpersonal interactions and themselves determine the course of these interactions in the future.

Again in a phenomenological vein, Adler attributes the control of behaviour to future goals rather than to mechanical driving forces as Freud does, and most of us would agree that any behaviour we engage in certainly *appears* to be directed towards some aim rather than to be instigated by a conglomeration of mechanical forces. In this sense Adler seems to be rejecting the mechanistic determinism accepted by psychoanalysts and replacing it by a teleological account of human activity. But Adler's teleology has been called 'immanent': a teleology in which the purpose, or final goal, of an organism is determined by the organism itself and not by some transcendental being, such as God, or by some pre-set indigenous plan.[5]

Like the existentialists, Adler places responsibility for behaviour in the individual; he leaves the behaver free to choose what he or she is going to do – to be active, not reactive to environmental or instinctual forces. Nevertheless, Adler embraced the principle of psychic determinism in the same sense as Freud did – that all psychological phenomena are meaningful. But the meaningfulness that Adlerians seek is in the future, in the goals of behaviour, not in the past. Ansbacher has referred to this as a historical determinism, and compared it to Allport's conception of functional autonomy.[6] In this respect, the difference between the clinicians, Adler and Freud, parallels that between the academicians, Allport and Eysenck.

It is conventional to regard mechanistic and purposive accounts of human behaviour as antithetical. Explanations of behaviour as dependent on historical contingencies of one kind or another appear to be incompatible with accounts of mankind that stress the purposive, goal-directed, striving into the future, side of human nature. Certainly for most purposes the second account appears to be correct. But appearance can deceive, for behaviour directed toward a goal is not necessarily divorced from historical control. A person turning a knob that opens a door may very well explain this action by appealing to the subsequent behaviour of entering the room: one opens the door because one so wishes, or because one intends to go into the room. But on further questioning the individual would have to admit that he or she turned the knob because in the past turning the knob had allowed the door to be opened.

I raise this question at this point to resolve the apparent contradiction between Adler's purposivism, which is ahistorical, and his attribution of an individual's life style to the constellation of circumstances involved in his or her childhood family interaction patterns, which is historical. This apparent contradiction may be resolved by appeal to a functional autonomy of motives, but only if a satisfactory and consistent account of how motives become functionally autonomous can be given, or by reference to historical sources of aspirations into the future. We may be less willing to attribute purpose, or forethought, to a pigeon than to a human, but if a pigeon is trained to peck at an illuminated disc five hundred times to obtain a grain of food, to all appearances the pigeon has a very definite goal in mind during the four hundred and ninety-nine unreinforced pecks. Possibly it has, but we do not explain the bird's behaviour by reference to its goal but by reference to the schedule of reinforcement on which it was trained.

Circumstances are likely to determine which kind of account, purposive or historical, is preferable. From the point of view of phenomenological introspection, the former would be the natural choice, but where the provenance of behaviour is in question the historical alternative is essential. It is from the standpoint of the scientific psychologist that I stress Adler's contribution to the theory of human behaviour as developing the situational variable approach to the control of behaviour. Phenomenologically he lies closer to the existentialists than to Freud, but functionally he is closest of all to the behaviourists.

Individual psychology has been described pejoratively as common-sense psychology, and Adler has been almost accused of intellectual cowardice on the ground that his writings and lectures have been directed more to the general public than to the intelligentsia. Sullivan, on the other hand, has suffered relative neglect through being too abstract and technical, although his sociological approach to infant development and adult personality has affinities with that of Adler.

Individual psychology and abnormal behaviour

Abnormal behaviour, to Adler's mind, is the expression of a faulty style of life – a style of life based on 'private' sense rather than on 'common' sense, in which self interest takes precedence over social interest. Adler places responsibility for this on the individual's social climate – one in which social interest fails to develop and an exaggerated sense of inferiority is acquired. Although the conditions that occasion inferiority feelings would also discourage the development of social interest,[7] Adler recognizes independent sources of inferiority, principally femininity and organ inferiority.

Because in the organization of Western societies there are biases in favour of males, females in general carry a greater load of inferiority. They are therefore faced with a social climate that is likely to generate excessive feelings of inferiority, and Adler claims to have noticed particular characteristics of female behaviour which he calls *masculine protest*. This phenomenon may be exhibited either by masculine, that is tom-boy, behaviour on the part of a girl, or by an exaggeration of feminine qualities. In the first case, the masculine challenge is met by masculine behaviour (if you can't beat 'em join 'em); in the second case, it is met by seduction – by attacking the male at his weakest point of defence. Either strategy would exemplify a style of life that, in Adler's terms, would only be abnormal if personal interest exceeded social interest and domination and superiority came to characterize the life style.

Organ inferiority refers to a physical defect that either lessens the individual's potential for appropriate social action, or reduces the likelihood of positive social responses to his or her behaviour. A child born with a specific disability, any kind of physical deformity, could not engage in the full range of normal childhood activity and thus would demonstrate inferiority in at least a few areas of behaviour. This could lead to excessive strivings for compensatory superiority in these or other spheres of activity. A child who is generally physically unattractive, and this does not exclude an individual with a particular deformity, is normally less likely to inspire love and affection in others than is an attractive child. Consequently the psychological climate in which the unattractive child grows up does not reinforce its normal growth of social interest. Its attempts to cope may take the form of strivings for superiority and dominance, which may successfully coerce sympathetic or guilt-ridden adults into complying with its demands.[8]

It is not difficult to see how both these conceptions – masculine protest and organ inferiority – can be encompassed within the framework of functional behaviourism. Whatever behaviour has reinforcing consequences will increase in probability, and if certain conditions, such as gender and deformity, make normally reinforced responses unlikely to occur, then these responses will atrophy in favour of others that eventually do attain reinforcement, even though they may not be intentionally or consciously performed.

The kinds of situational conditions that Adler especially stresses as producers of abnormal feelings of inferiority are both overindulgence and neglectful treatment of the child by its parents. The overprotected pampered child may come to feel inferior because it is continually reminded of its inability to act independently. Also, because its normal needs are met by its mother's actions rather than by its own, the ordinary childhood skills may go unacquired through lack of opportunity and experience. Neglectfulness, on the other hand, particularly if accompanied by active denigration, resentfulness, and even hatred, can also be expected to lead to feelings of inferiority unless the child has means of coping with its environment beyond the family circle. The total mental picture of the world that the child develops as a result of all these conditions Adler called the *apperceptive scheme*. This is the child's subjective, private view of the world, and the perception that colours the style of life that the child uses to cope with, or overcome it.

The principal behaviour problems that Adler and his followers have considered are problem children, criminals and delinquents, alcoholics and drug addicts, sexual perverts and prostitutes, neurotics and psychotics, all of whom are characterized as differing from normality – in degree, by virtue of exaggerated feelings of inferiority, and in kind, according to their particular forms of faulty compensatory behaviour.

These compensations, or overcompensations, are unique to each individual, but the circumstances that generate them Adler traces to the universal problems of inferiority and social interest. Like the behaviourists, he believes that the laws of behaviour govern normal and abnormal conditions alike, and that it is only the social context of his or her upbringing that turns one individual into a criminal and another into a judge.[9] The one has acquired a faulty style of private interest and the other a normal style of public interest. So far as the abnormal individual is concerned, Adler is insistent that what has happened in his or her life is not something that *had* to happen but something that *could* have happened and, given the circumstances, could have happened to anyone. This is the spirit in which the Adlerian approaches psychotherapy.

The general aspects of abnormal behaviour, Adler calls *neurotic safeguards*. These safeguards are ways in which the abnormal personality maintains its fiction of superiority. They take the forms of *aggression* and *seeking distance*, which can be seen as reactions to a world that has fostered excessive feelings of inferiority on the one hand, and has failed to foster social interest on the other. Aggressive, superiority-directed behaviour may appear as depreciation of others, and so as enhancement of oneself; as self-abasement, in which the blame for one's own condition is attributed to others; as attachment to excessively high ideals and aspirations that most people could not live up to; and as any other activity that serves to ameliorate the neurotic's inferior position.

Seeking distance is withdrawing from social contacts by avoiding or escaping from them, by flight or by excuse, and by restricting contact with the world to those areas in which personal fantasies of superiority are unlikely to be challenged. The individual adjusts by reducing his level of activity. Adler, like some existentialists and behaviourists, does not consider abnormal behaviour to be maladjusted but as adjusted to a peculiar set of unfortunate circumstances. The child is improperly prepared for social interaction in the beginning; it adjusts as best it can by seeking distance from people and by maintaining its sense of security by preserving itself from challenge.

Particular situational variables

Because the circumstances surrounding any individual life are unique, it is difficult to point to any particular set of conditions responsible for certain styles of living. Nevertheless, there are some general characteristics to be found as factors in most lives, and these appear in the context of family structure. The dangers of parental overindulgence or rejection and neglect have already been considered, but Adler also gives attention to the matter of position in the family. Birth order he regards as important, not because this as such is responsible for certain personality characteristics, but because the child's position in the family necessitates certain interpersonal relationships that raise the probability of one kind of behaviour over another.

The oldest child, for example, enjoys a relationship with its parents that younger siblings can never obtain. As it can only lose its autonomous position it is reasonable to anticipate that it will develop a style of life centred on authority and defensiveness against competition. The second child, however, must compete aggressively if it is to attain a position of equality with its elder brother or sister. It begins life as inferior not only to its parents but also to a rival for their attention. It is, says Adler, less likely to accept the sanctity of authority, but to become nonconformist if it meets with success, or defeatist and cynical if it does not. The youngest child in the family is never faced with competition from below, and if it is treated as the family baby is likely to grow up in this image – egocentric, weak and incompetent. None of these syndromes is inevitable, however, and factors such as family size and spacing, changing parental skills and habits – even economic circumstances – can easily override the general pattern.

There is an extra factor to be considered in the case of the only child – the possibility of its being unwanted. In this case, there would be a high probability that it would be faced with hostile and rejecting parental attitudes. Without this eventuality the only child would resemble the youngest in a larger family insofar as it is spoiled and pampered. But it has a further potential disadvantage to the extent that it is cut off from other children for a while, open only to adult control and influence in its infancy.

Other areas of relative social consistency are schooling and marriage. Adler did not specify how these might shape personality. He was chiefly concerned with reforming the school atmosphere away from one concerned with rigidity and discipline towards one more conducive to growth and positive feelings than to fear and hostility. But inasmuch as he regarded the foundations of personality as fully established in the pre-school years, the circumstances of schooling and adult interpersonal relationships commanded less attention from him than did the earlier social climate of childhood.

Adlerian psychotherapy

Many of Adler's notions about human nature are similar to those held by the existentialists, and many of his recommendations about therapy are in accord with the precepts of functional behaviourism. So there is a sense in which Adler, who has had relatively little influence on the philosophy and practices of psychiatrists and clinical psychologists, bridges the apparent gulf between two salient schools of thought in contemporary psychology and psychiatry.

Adlerian concepts that are also fundamental to existentialism are as follows:

- *The creative self.* The notion that humans do not simply react to the result of the interplay of libidinal forces but actively choose the way they behave. In both systems the choice is coloured by the social context of a particular life.
- *Expectations.* The notion that behaviour is determined not by the past but by goals established for the future.
- *Subjectivity.* The claim that individuals behave according to what they subjectively believe to be true and not according to what actually is true; although Adlerians are more willing to talk of a patient's mistakes, or errors, than are the existentialists.
- *Style of life.* The concept by which Adler emphasizes the uniqueness of each individual and the unity of his or her personality, which needs to be understood rather than explained.
- *Adjustment.* The recognition that abnormal behaviour is not mal-adjusted, in the sense of being inappropriate to its social context, but is actually an adjustment to prevailing conditions of living, and that this adjustment is accomplished by a restriction in the life sphere of the individual.
- *Social interest.* The conception that individuals exist in relation to their communities, and that a personality evolves according to the success or failure of a person's interpersonal relationships.
- *Superiority strivings.* The idea that the individual strives to contend with the world rather than be victimized by it. This idea has similar connotations to the existential concept of self-actualization, the striving to become. This striving may take the wrong direction and be expressed as self-centred power seeking, which is equivalent to the existential level of gaining security through exploitation.
- *The unconscious.* The notion that people do not know everything there is to be known about themselves. The unconscious is not a repository of behaviour-directing forces.

With these commonalities, it is not surprising that Adler's *general* view of psychotherapy corresponds with those of the existentialists. As existentialists require the therapist and patient to share a common existence, so Adler wishes them to share a common set of values; as existentialists endeavour to accept patients for what they are instead of for what they ought to be, so Adler recognizes that what has happened to the patient could have happened to any one. As he says,

Everything which happened did not have to happen in such a way necessarily, but, under the circumstances *could* happen; and if we are able to feel with the child, to think with him, and conclude that under the same conditions, and with the same mistaken goal of a *personal* superiority, we would have acted in much the same way.[10]

When it comes to the specifics of guidance and psychotherapy, Adler makes use of principles of behaviour advocated by the functional behaviourists, although there has been no material cross-fertilization between Adlerian and Skinnerian schools of thought.

From studies of animal behaviour in the laboratory, functional behaviourists have discovered that modification of behaviour is better accomplished by positive reinforcement than by punishment, and that it is possible to shape behaviour in small steps when more gross requirements cannot be met. From his experience in the psychological clinic, Adler recommends encouragement rather than punishment, and that alternative goals to the fictional ones that the patient already has should not be set so high that he or she cannot, in the beginning, attain them. Likewise, both schools recognize that behaviour is maintained by agencies outside the individual, and that psychotherapy requires not only attention to the person who happens to be called the patient but also to the close circle of acquaintances, particularly the family of that patient.

Another point of contact between Adlerian and Skinnerian psychologies is in the treatment of dependency behaviour. A child who clings to its mother's skirts is often thought of as in need of security. The treatment for this would be for the mother to give the child all the reassurance and unconditional love that she can. The usual assumption is that the more indulgence and pampering the child receives the sooner will its excessive need be met and its behaviour return to normal. This approach is in contrast to the behaviourist's reinforcement theory, with which Adler is in accord. From this standpoint, grovelling behaviour is maintained because this is the behaviour to which the mother attends. Very often it is the only way the child can attract her, and as attention is a powerful reinforcer, the very behaviour that the mother wishes to extinguish she is inadvertently strengthening. The solution, according to both Adlerian and behavioural therapies, is to withdraw attention from dependency behaviour and transfer it to more suitable activity, particularly by encouragement and praise for self-reliance.

Insofar as abnormal behaviour is the exemplification of personal interest at the expense of social interest, the goal of Adlerian therapy is to reverse this inequality. To do this, the therapist must *understand* the patient and explain this understanding so that the patient comes to share it. Understanding in this case may be equated with insight on the part of the patient. However it is not the same kind of insight and understanding as that sought by orthodox psychoanalysts. Freudian analysts equate insight with exposing the unconscious by means of interpretations of symbols that serve to *disguise* its intentions. To Adlerians, insight is the extension of one's breadth of awareness about the functions of one's behaviour through interpretations of what the symbols in one's expressive behaviour and dreams are *expressing*.

Because social interest was originally curbed by family mother-child relationships, the therapist may play the role of the 'ideal mother'. Adler recommends that the therapist pay close attention to the patient, have genuine sympathy, and refrain from hostility, criticism, and moral judgement. The therapist as a person must have a highly developed social interest, and it is this, more than the therapist's technical knowledge, that is most important. Unlike the passive psychoanalyst, the Adlerian actively engages in social commerce with the client, and it is precisely the therapist's sensitivity in this interchange that determines the course of therapy.

Of course, Adler gives some technical advice, including the utilization of encouragement over punishment, and the restriction of goals to those that can reasonably be achieved. In the language of the functional behaviourists, the therapist aims to become a social reinforcer for the client so that the client develops feelings of competency rather than incompetency, and begins to act with people rather than against them. This would happen as a result of positive reinforcement generalized from rewarding interactions with the therapist.

In Adlerian therapy the patient is required to conceal nothing from the therapist, to trust and like him or her, and to come to accept the therapist's values and ways of perceiving the world.[11] But these cannot be achieved by fiat. If the therapist is socially sensitive and has a sufficient store of social interest, then there is no need to demand compliance from the patient on those points. The social reinforcing power of the therapist is enough to free the behaviour of the patient from the constraints imposed by a non-reinforcing community.

Finally, on diagnosis: as the laws of abnormal behaviour are taken to be the same as those of normal behaviour, formal psychiatric diagnosis has no place in Adler's system. Psychological failure (unless directly the result of organic defect) is a result of underdeveloped social interest expressed as a particular style of life. But there are many ways in which social interest may be curbed. These are investigated by means of an *individualizing examination* in which childhood memories of possible aggravating life conditions, like organ inferiority and intra-family rivalries are recovered, either directly or through accounts of dreams and other more or less oblique communications. It is in the individualizing examination that the variables occasioning and maintaining a patient's difficulties are sought.

Interpersonal psychiatry

Whereas Alfred Adler broke away from the Vienna Psychoanalytic Society to begin a new, anti-Freudian, approach to the theory and technique of psychotherapy, the second wave of psychoanalysts with a sociological orientation have been called not anti-Freudian, but neo-Freudian. The best known neo-Freudians are Karen Horney and Erich Fromm (whose major writings are more existential than psychoanalytic), but the most elaborate and detailed revisions of psychoanalytic theory were by Harry Stack Sullivan, the leading figure of the Washington School of Psychiatry from the early 1930s until his death in 1949.

Like Adler, Sullivan emphasized the young infant's helplessness and his striving for power, and by power meant not dominance over people but accomplishment or collaboration with them. Like Adler, he stressed the social role of the mother in the creation of the infant's personality. But he went very much further than Adler in his emphasis on the interpersonal nature of behaviour and adopted a position not inconsistent with that of the functional behaviourists.

Skinner and Sullivan both attribute behaviour to the effects of interpersonal relationships; Skinner in the notion of the reinforcing community and Sullivan by reference to the self as the reflected appraisals of significant others. Both eliminate the O-variable as a storehouse for cognitions, ideas or personalities. On the interdependence of an organism and its environment, Sullivan gives the following illustration:

> Every seventh-grade grammar school boy, I am sure, knows that oxygen is a gas which is an ingredient of the atmosphere and that this gas is in some fashion vital to life. It is a very clever seventh-grade boy who knows that oxygen gets out of the atmosphere into the body and is presently returned to the atmosphere in the shape of carbon dioxide; but what very few seventh-grade pupils know, and some fourth-year medical students have not yet quite captured, is the notion that there is very little storage of oxygen and that life is dependent on the continual, almost uninterrupted, exchange between the oxygen of the atmosphere, the oxygen in the body, the carbon dioxide in the body and in the atmosphere.[12]

A conversation and a duel are psychological examples of transactions without storage. In a conversation, stored ideas are not passed back and forth between speakers,[13] nor do the participants in a duel exchange thrusts and parries drawn from a behavioural repository.[14]

The definition of personality

Sullivan[15] explicitly defines personality as *'The relatively enduring pattern of recurrent interpersonal situations which characterize a human life'*, thereby reducing the conventional account of personality as a uniquely organized system of O-variables within the organism to vanishing point.[16] It is true that Sullivan did acknowledge a 'true or absolute individuality of a person' but regarded it as 'always beyond scientific grasp and invariably much less significant in the person's living than he has been taught to believe'.[17] What he did regard as significant is the interactions between people, because these are the events that the scientist observes. If we think of these events as conforming to 'trajectories' (see note 16), individuality may not always be as far beyond scientific grasp as Sullivan believed.

So, by Sullivan's definition, personality, or at least what is scientifically significant about personality, does not exist in isolation but only in interaction. Moreover, the development of characteristic behaviours, he says, comes about according to the pattern of rewards and punishments encountered in interpersonal activities:

> The infant plays, one might say, the old game of getting hotter or colder, in charting a selection of behavioral units which are not attended by an increase in anxiety.[18]

This is not unlike Skinner's conception of behaviour shaped by contingent reinforcement, but Skinner puts more emphasis on the power of positive reinforcement while Sullivan concerns himself chiefly with the effects of negative reinforcement – the removal of anxiety – on the control of behaviour. In this sense, Sullivan follows Freud's stress on the shaping of behaviour (defence mechanisms) by aversive events.

There are important differences between Skinner and Sullivan. Skinner has developed his research through detailed investigations of the conditions of reinforcement, particularly schedules of reinforcement, while Sullivan has described the different sources of reinforcement – significant others – in a person's life. Also, whereas Skinner has consistently refused to deal with an O-variable at all as pertinent to the control of behaviour, Sullivan went on to construct a metaphorical O. However, even here the similarities outweigh the differences between them, because both Skinner and Sullivan construct consciousness on the basis of verbal behaviour developed out of interpersonal interactions, and both acknowledge that verbal behaviour is an important source of self-control. But this does not mean that *the* self is a set of wishes, impulses, instinctual forces, or whatever, which exert control over action, or that there is a personality that initiates behaviour.

One reason that it is difficult to accept or understand Sullivan's definition of personality in its literal sense, is that it is customary to approach the problem of personality from one's own rather than from a companion's point of view. Yet we would agree that people behave quite differently in some types of company from the way they do in others. Some people we find amusing, to many we are indifferent, and some bore us to the limit. In all these instances we think of ourselves as 'I' who am happy, indifferent or bored and that the 'I' is a fixed, immutable personality exposed to other equally immutable personalities at different times.

We seldom stop to see ourselves as we might be seen, but it is certain that we would be described differently by our friends and by people who do not enjoy our company. We behave differently according to the company we happen to be keeping, and we should not expect to be described in the same way by all our acquaintances. It might seem that one's own account would best describe one's 'real personality', but in that case, why are there psychologists and psychiatrists whose job it is to measure personality or change it?

It is not hard to persuade individuals to select a personality sketch that matches themselves – 'the real me'. If they are then given a different sketch and asked to name someone who sees them like *that* they might readily do so, and even repeat the performance through a number of sketches. We describe ourselves one way, our self-image, but can see ourselves differently from other points of view while still maintaining the fiction of 'the real me'. From the outside we behave as though personality were interpersonal – a matrix of characteristics typifying the interactions between two or more persons – but from the inside we do not. One behaves as though one's personality is one's own, is oneself and has nothing to do with the company one keeps.

I have not presented this example as a statement of Sullivan's views but as a slightly overdrawn account that I hope will make his definition of personality intelligible. As a matter of fact, Sullivan does not particularly allow for the multiplicity of personalities that I have described, for he refers to the 'relatively *enduring pattern* of *recurrent* interpersonal situations ...' and it is from these that the individual *personifies* himself. He comes to see himself as a particular kind of person because there are recurring patterns of interpersonal situations in which he typically interacts in more or less similar ways, and it is from these that, sooner or later, he personifies himself in a particular, characteristic way.

The personification of the self develops according to different kinds of interpersonal situations that occur in a person's life. Like Freud, Sullivan conceived of a number of stages in development before maturity: infancy, childhood, juvenile, preadolescence, early and late adolescence. However, he thought of these not as a series of staging posts through which intrapsychic forces pass, but as eras in life in which different interpersonal factors come into play, in which the individual interacts with an expanding and changing circle of *significant others*.

In infancy (from birth to the onset of speech), the principal significant other is the infant's mother, and the chief mode of interaction is by bodily contact. The stage of childhood lasts from the beginning of speech to the time the child starts to engage in social play. In this stage, the child assimilates the basic rules of society. In the next, the juvenile phase, the child's world is enlarged still further to include other authorities than its parents, particularly teachers. In this stage, the juvenile moves from casual to more intimate friendships. In the behaviourist's language, the young person enlarges his or her reinforcement community, and may find that behaviour reinforced in one community (the home) proves inadequate in another (the school) and *vice versa*. The pre-, early and late adolescent periods are characterized by attachment to friends, infatuation and lust, and love respectively.

The development of the self

The self is the metaphorical O-variable in Sullivan's system, but it is basically no more than the interpersonal experience of the individual: 'The peculiarity of the self is that it may be said to be made up of *reflected appraisals*' or in words even closer to those of the behaviourists: 'The self dynamism is built up out of this experience of approbation and approval, of reward and punishment.'[19]

The 'this experience' that Sullivan is referring to is the outcome of behaviour directed toward the *pursuit of satisfaction* and the *maintenance of security*. The pursuit of satisfaction refers to behaviour that originates in biological tension, the need for food and water, for example, and is satisfied by reduction or removal of these tensions. The individual is said to learn whatever actions result in tension reduction, a point of view held by some behaviourists.[20] The maintenance of security, however, is more concerned with the psychological well-being of the individual, and is governed by the appeasement of others rather than oneself. Anxiety, according to Sullivan, is the loss of security, and in the normal process of socialization, as felt anxiety is alleviated security is gained.

There are clear affinities between these notions of satisfaction and security needs and Freud's pleasure and reality principles. Freud imagined that the human infant began life with a set of psychological energies that he called the id, and that the ego developed out of this primary system as a result of the infant's contacts with reality. The id, he believed, operated entirely on the basis of pleasure, but the ego was acknowledged to submit to the dictates of the outside world, so far as it could under pressure from the id. When the infant engaged in outrageous id-dominated behaviour it was the ego that suffered the brunt of counter-attack; the sufferings of the ego were related directly to the antics of the id.

Sullivan did not invent mental forces to account for the phenomena that id and ego appear to explain, but he did observe the behavioural phenomena in very much the same way as Freud had, even to the extent of recognizing that security operations are shaped as a consequence of behaviour utilized in the pursuit of satisfactions. Moreover, he related satisfaction to bodily zones, particularly the oral, anal and genital – the same areas that Freud thought of as particularly important to the id.

To Sullivan, the self-system (ego) is a secondary dynamism that is 'purely the result of interpersonal experience arising from anxiety encountered in the pursuit of the satisfaction of general and zonal needs'.[21] The emphasis is on the self as a result of interpersonal relations, not on the elaboration of a given biological intrapsychic energy.

Like satisfaction, security is maintained or lost according to the mother's approval or disapproval, reward or punishment of the infant's behaviour, and Sullivan describes how the mother comes to shape her child's behaviour by her reactions to it. At first, according to Sullivan, the good mother treats her child with tenderness and affection in tending to its needs for satisfaction. But, as

> the infant comes to be recognized as educable, capable of learning, the mothering one modifies more and more the exhibition of tenderness, or the giving of tenderness, to the infant. The earlier feeling that the infant must have unqualified cooperation is now modified to the feeling that the infant should be learning certain things, and this implies a restriction, on the part of the mothering one, of her tender cooperation under certain circumstances.

Sullivan goes on:

> tenderness as a sequel to what the mothering one regards as good behavior ... is, in effect – however it may be prehended by the infant – a *reward* ...[22]

To this, Sullivan adds that the parent may react tenderly or neutrally towards the child's behaviour (and here he is talking particularly about activity centered around the anal zone, for example, toilet training) without any deliberate thought of rewarding the child. That is, he recognizes, like Adler and the behaviourists, that rewards and punishments are operating in the control of human behaviour even though the recipient may be unaware that he or she is being rewarded and the reinforcing community may not be intentionally dispensing or withholding reward.[23]

In general, there is a progression from the behaviourists through Adler to Sullivan in their emphasis on the extent of operation of reinforcement, or reward. The behaviourists, because the bulk of their work has been with animals and with the mechanical delivery of reward, have given most attention to the effect of reinforcement on the overt motor response that produces it, and relatively less to the reinforcement delivery mechanisms or the organism's attitude to itself. Adler, on the other hand, has emphasized the effect of the reinforcing person on the developing child's attitude to people in general; this is his notion of social interest. And Adler sets relatively more store on the behaviour that is learned toward the reinforcing agent than on the behaviour that is strengthened by it. Sullivan goes one step further. He acknowledges that reward controls the behaviour that produces it, that the child forms attitudes towards the reinforcing agent – the *good mother* and the *bad mother*, according to when she dispenses rewards or generates anxiety – but he also stresses the prehensions that the child develops about itself – the *good me*, the *bad me*. By its security operations the child learns to behave in certain ways, but it also personifies others and itself: it develops a *self dynamism*.

I do not wish to imply that Sullivan has dealt with concepts that Adler and the behaviourists have ignored, but only to indicate the areas of interest that have been most emphasized by the respective theoretical systems. All three systems do, in fact, have something to say about all three functions of reward that I have mentioned. The behaviourists, for example, have considered attitudes toward the reinforcing agent (although they would not phrase it that way) in their concept of generalized secondary reinforcement, and have shown that organisms will work to produce stimuli that signal the eventuality of primary reinforcement. This state of affairs could be regarded as demonstrating the organism's liking for the reinforcing mechanism, although the behaviourists would not regard the notion of 'liking' as adding anything to the understanding of behaviour. Likewise, Skinner[24] has analysed the concept of self in behavioural terms, and his account of verbal behaviour[25] incorporates the person's statements about his or her own behaviour – about self dynamisms, in other words.

At first, according to Sullivan, lost security is regained by escape from anxiety generated by the 'mothering one'. This anxiety, Sullivan has claimed, is acquired through empathy or induction. Empathy is the infant's only means of interpersonal contact. It is its non-verbal sensing of the attitudes of significant others towards the things it does. Accordingly, the child understands by way of 'emotional contagion' whether the mother approves or disapproves of its conduct, which means that when the infant generates anxiety in the mother the infant's anxiety level is also raised through induction. An example would be the mother's concern when the infant raises inedible or dangerous objects to its mouth. As the child chews or sucks on the forbidden object the mother's anxiety is raised and, as a result, so is the infant's. In this way, anxiety may become dynamically centered on the *oral zone*.

Escape from anxiety is beyond the child's personal power for, unlike behaviour that satisfies needs, the infant has no innate ways of relieving anxiety. Such relief can come about only as the situation changes, and the mother loses her anxiety, either as a result of something the child does, or for some other reason. But ultimately, the child learns to attend to the cues that signal impending approbation, what Sullivan calls *selective attention*, and to behave in ways that avoid anxiety and maintain security.

An alternative way of avoiding anxiety is *selective inattention* to situations that produce it, with the result that part of the self is *disassociated*, or split off from consciousness. The phenomenon of disassociation resembles repression, but Sullivan does not involve competing ego and instinctual forces in the process for he postulates no instinct to be repressed. At its simplest level, selective inattention is akin to discrimination; the child simply comes to ignore events that it cannot control or objects it cannot have.

There are times when the need for satisfaction conflicts with the need for security. At first, satisfaction is all that matters to the child, and this need must be met if the child is to survive. But socialization is basically the opposition of satisfaction by security, and ultimately security becomes more powerful. That is to say, anxiety over loss of security comes to outweigh satisfaction needs, which must temporarily be held in abeyance. This conflict is reminiscent of the battle between the superego and the id for control over the ego. The need for satisfaction corresponds to id forces, and that for security to the superego. Personal needs cannot be satisfied willy-nilly in civilized society, and both Freud and Sullivan agree that anxiety plays an important part in the socialization process. To Freud, the ego is something that instinctual and social forces struggle to control, it is a separate thing, but to Sullivan the self is the outcome of the individual's contact with society, and not a separate, more or less independent O-variable acting in its own right. In the last analysis, where Freud sees behavioural complexities through complex intrapsychic dynamics, Sullivan sees them as the interplay of complex interpersonal transactions.

Dynamisms: zonal needs and general needs

Sullivan defines dynamism as *'The relatively enduring pattern of energy transformations which recurrently characterize the organism in its duration as a living organism.'*[26] He arrives at this definition by way of the general scientific notion that the ultimate reality in the universe is energy, a consequence of Einstein's Special Theory of Relativity. The following imaginary conversation is a phenomenological illustration of the point:

> A friend of mine owns a desk at which he writes and on which his friends sit and spill cigarette ashes. An inquiry about the real nature of the desk had the following results:
> 'It is really cellulose.'
> 'What is that?'

'A molecular combination of carbon, hydrogen, and oxygen.'
'What are they?'
'They are made up of protons and electrons.'
'What are they?'
'They are really charges of electricity.'
'What are they?'
'They are not matter, just waves.'
'What are they?'
'Not waves in anything, just waves.'
'What are they?'
'All right, waves of nothing!'[27]

It is a long stride from sub-atomic physics to psychology and
psychiatry, but what Sullivan is driving at is this: the most obvious
facts of the universe are material objects, and our dealings with
things that are immaterial are coloured by our pervasive acquaintance with and interest in the material. Consequently there is a
strong tendency for us to reify, or at least give the appearance of
reification, in our treatment of psychological phenomena. Thus,
mind, experience, id, ego, superego, instincts, drives, wishes and so
on, are commonly thought of as 'things', albeit different things from
tables, chairs, trees, ash-trays and the like. But psychological
things are not objects and it is dangerous to speak of them as if they
were, in the sense of having some kind of peculiar spatial quality.
As tangible objects are expressible in energy as well as mass terms
($E = mc^2$), so psychological phenomena can be conceptualized as
patterns of energy transformations without recourse to metaphorical reification.

It is easy to mistake Sullivan's meaning and regard his concept
of dynamisms as logically similar to the Freudian mechanisms,
mechanisms that stand behind, or are responsible for, the functional activity of the organism. To Sullivan dynamism *is* the
functional activity of the organism, and when he speaks of sub-
dynamism he is speaking of classes or patterns of functional activities organized around some particular centre of interest. The self
dynamism is the concatenation of sub-dynamisms appearing in any
particular individual.

Dynamisms may be organized around particular anatomical
zones or they may occur in a more general way. The difference
between zonal and general needs roughly parallels the distinction

between needs for satisfaction and for security. As we have seen, needs for satisfaction – zonal needs – are primary, while those for security are secondary, in the sense that they are aroused as a result of difficulties encountered in the pursuit of satisfaction.

The zonal needs that Sullivan mentions are oral, anal and urethral. These are bodily zones involved in the physical requirements of eating and drinking, excreting, urinating and procreating. Anxiety and fear are tension dynamisms arising from disjunctive interpersonal relations encountered in pursuing satisfaction of zonal needs. Zonal dynamisms are the behavioural patterns acquired through interpersonal relationships encountered during activities relevant to the respective anatomical zones.

Other needs that Sullivan considers to be important are those for intimacy and lust. Unlike Freud, Sullivan considers the lust dynamism to be relatively dormant before adolescence, and to play a significant part in rectifying mistakes in living that may have occurred in growing up. Another tension, loneliness, is the result of failure to satisfy the need for intimacy, and is taken by Sullivan to be almost as debilitating an experience as anxiety. It is a need that changes its object in time, and will be considered again in the discussion of developmental eras below.

The child's modes of experiencing

The problem of how the child communicates with significant others, and how it receives and prehends information from them is examined more closely by Sullivan than by Adler.

In their order of development, the major communicating and experiencing channels that Sullivan recognizes are *empathy*, *prototaxis*, *parataxis*, *autism* and *language* (syntaxis). These refer to the thoughts or feelings of the child as a result of its interactions with significant others. They are the modes of the child's experiences as it grows up, the picture of the world and of itself that it acquires through communication with significant others.

Empathy, as I have said, is the infant's first sensing of the anxiety or tenderness of the mothering adult. It is of principal importance in the interpersonal contacts of the infant up to about two years of age, for it is the only way it can sense the feelings of others towards itself. Even at this early age, the child is thought to experience anxiety when it senses disapproval, although it is not yet able to call upon established behaviours that escape or avoid anxiety.

From a simple empathic relationship to the world, the infant passes through a diffuse prototaxic phase to a parataxic conception of events. In the prototaxic mode, Sullivan infers, the infant's feelings simply occur. They carry no meaning, and the infant's total experience is only a temporal sequence of unconnected happenings. The prototaxic mode is pre-symbolic, in the sense that nothing stands for, or is a sign of, anything else; there is no recall of order that might have gone before, or foresight of what might possibly come.

Passage into the parataxic mode of experience is indicated by a differentiation of experience into connected events, but with no comprehension of relationships between them: one thing just happens to be a sign that another event will occur, but the child's experience is not of a logical, or quasi-logical connection between them. Events are experienced as occurring in a mechanical, purely arbitrary way. The meaningful relationships between happenings, causes and effects, are missed. In the parataxic mode the child may recognize that A goes with B, but the necessary functional relationship between them is not cognized. The connection is arbitrary, and the symbolization of one thing by another is private and personal.[28]

The parataxic mode continues through the beginning of language acquisition. At first, says Sullivan, use of language is autistic; it is personal and private, although personal and private here mean interpersonal and private to the child and some significant other. That is, the meaning of a word or sound produced by a child is the behaviour of some listener to this sound, and if the listener responds consistently to a nonsensical noise then this is what the noise means so far as the child is concerned. As Sullivan puts it, 'Words do not carry meaning, but evoke meaning.'[29] They occasion some response on the part of the listener, which is also Skinner's view.

In fact, most of the work with animals undertaken by the behaviourists assumes parataxic experience on the part of their subjects. When an animal performs some act that is followed by reinforcement, the repetition of this act by the animal is not taken as an indication that the animal understands the nature of the situation.[30] The operation of reinforcement is said to be enough to strengthen behaviour, and the behaviourist does not assume that any cognitive intervention takes place, unless it is cognitive behaviour that obeys whatever laws govern overt motor events.[31]

Although Sullivan carries the human mode of experience beyond the parataxic into the syntaxic, where 'normal' linguistic understanding and communication obtains, no new mechanism is involved, for the public use of language extends beyond the private use by means of what Sullivan has called *consensual validation*. Groups of people now begin to respond similarly to certain expressions which previously had evoked reactions in only a limited audience. But Sullivan also adds the element of understanding to the syntaxic mode of experience, as though some insight into the true meaning of events transcends the principles of interpersonal consensual validation. Learning, he maintains, takes place by trial and error and success, where behaviour (including speech) may be initiated by rising anxiety or by a human model, and also by *eduction* in the sense used by Spearman.[32] It is this third kind of learning, which appears to be a private discovery in so far as the individual educes a heretofore unexpected relationship, that may not require the intervention of another person, either as a model or as a reinforcing agent who serves to reduce anxiety.

Actually, Sullivan believes that vast areas of human experience do not occur in the syntaxic mode at all, but exist as *parataxic distortions*. In particular, these refer to the false attribution to strangers of characteristics and attitudes of significant others in an individual's personal history. The individual sees people not as they really are, but as fantasied personages from the past. The concept refers to the same kind of phenomena that the psychoanalysts call transference, although there is no similarity between transference and parataxic distortions as explanatory mechanisms.

Stages of human development

So far, Sullivan's theory has been described very much as it relates to the way in which a person becomes who he or she is, but very little has been said about the descriptive side of Sullivan's system – what a person might become, and what kinds of interpersonal incidents might influence her or him. Sullivan had a great deal to say on this account.

Almost every theorist about personality has something to say about the way things typically turn out. They make astute observations on how people behave, as well as guess reasons for these behaviours, and Sullivan was no exception. But he was aware that things do not have to be the way they are, and like Adler, Watson and the functional behaviourists, he stressed that people could be very different from the way we normally see them:

> So far as I know most of the ways in which one goes about being a human being could be very different from everything we have ever heard of. In other words, the human organism is so extraordinarily adaptive that not only could the most fantastic social modes and regulations be lived up to, if they were properly inculcated in the young, but they would seem very natural and proper ways of life ...[33]

What human organisms become depends upon the treatment they receive during the various eras of life.

Infancy

Freud paid very little attention to the details of infant behaviour himself, although some of his followers, Melanie Klein in particular, were very concerned about the lives of very young babies. Even so, within the psychoanalytic tradition no one has been so attentive to the living conditions of the very young infant as Sullivan, and he devotes more discussion to this phase of life than to any other, although most of it is inferential rather than observational.

A prime characteristic of the new born infant, and for many months after birth, is its helplessness. The human infant *must* lead an interpersonal life for it could not survive otherwise, and almost its only source of interpersonal contact is with its mother, or a mother substitute.[34] Consequently what the infant comes to know of the world – empathically, prototaxically and parataxically – depends very much upon her. She satisfies its biological needs and manages to maintain its state of euphoria by administering tenderness, or to activate its security operations.

Sullivan states two theorems pertinent to the relationship between mother and child, the *Theorem of Tenderness* and the *Theorem of Anxiety*. According to the first, tension in the infant provokes tenderness in the mother; according to the second, anxiety in the mother induces anxiety in the child. Actually the first theorem requires, and contains, behavioural statements, for it is 'the observed activity of the infant arising from the tension of needs' that impels the mother 'to activities toward the relief of the infant's needs'. These infantile needs are entirely physico-chemical tensions like hunger, thirst, and so on. They are relieved when the mother feeds or changes the infant.

The observed activity of the infant is, of course, crying, and here Sullivan distinguishes crying-when-hungry from crying-when-cold. That is, crying-when-hungry and crying-when-cold are not the same thing for the infant even though the two cries may sound very much alike. The meaning of a communication, it will be remembered, is not something carried in the communication but is determined by the reaction of an audience – and the audience reaction is very different when a nipple is placed in the mouth from when a diaper is changed.

Once again, despite differences in terminology and in areas of focal interest, there is an affinity between the views of Sullivan and Skinner, because in his account of verbal behaviour Skinner too recognizes that the same objective behaviour can be under more than one source of control (see Chapter 6). For example, the word 'water' may be used as a *mand*, as in a sentence where water is 'demanded', or as a *tact*, as in a sentence where water is named. In the first case, utterance of the word is reinforced by the bringing of water, while in the second the reinforcement is by approval. Likewise the occasioning stimuli, thirst in the one case and the objective presence of water in the other, are also different. The same objective response, then, can be occasioned by different stimuli and reinforced in different ways, corresponding to Sullivan's notions of crying-when-hungry and crying-when-cold – crying satisfied, respectively, by food and warmth.

Of course, the infant's needs are not always satisfactorily met by the mother. Sometimes crying may go unheeded. This may be because the mother is occupied with other business or because she believes it is not feeding time. Or sometimes her own anxiety may upset the child, as the second theorem states. The result is different in the two cases.

In the first case, when crying-when-hungry does not produce food, when the normal response to hunger does not work, Sullivan postulates a mounting anxiety in the child which produces apathy and finally sleep. Such an occasion of failure of behaviour to produce its normal consequence Sullivan refers to as a *negative instance* or an infrequent event. However, infrequent negative events do not, he says, have much effect: 'The erasing effect of negative experience is not very impressive, even from extremely early in life.'[35] The immediate effect is apathy, but the unsatisfied behaviour soon regains its strength and may persist into later life. As Sullivan says, 'Unnumbered negative instances can be overlooked for years in the area of one's more acute personal problems.'[36]

Once again Sullivan through clinical observation has hit upon a phenomenon that has been extensively studied in the animal laboratory – schedules of reinforcement.[37] Numerous studies of animal behaviour have shown that responses can be maintained when reinforcement occurs infrequently – when, in fact, the infrequent negative instances that Sullivan talks about are much more common than positive, reinforcing consequences. Such reinforcement schedules are described in detail in Chapter 5. They are formal statements of dynamic interpersonal environments that contrast with Freud's dynamic structure of the psyche.

The second way in which the mother may fail to satisfy her infant's needs is when she herself becomes anxious while she is feeding it. This anxiety need not result from the child's behaviour – Sullivan uses as an example anxiety generated in the mother on receiving a telegram – but, of course, the infant is not aware of this. According to the second theorem, the mother's anxiety arouses anxiety in the child, and as anxiety is hypothesized to interfere with the child's feeding behaviour further anxiety is generated in the mother, and so on in a vicious circle. The child's satisfaction for feeding is not met, and anxiety mounts doubly in mother and child. Insofar as it is able, the infant relates this anxiety to its own behaviour vis-à-vis the oral zone even though the mother's anxiety may be externally aroused. There is no need for a consequence to occur *because* of some preceding activity for the consequence to have an effect on that activity, mere temporal contiguity is enough.

Skinner[38] has made the same claim on the basis of laboratory data gathered with pigeons.

Now, although it is the same objective nipple that accompanies satisfactory and unsatisfactory feedings, Sullivan infers that the infant is unaware of this and senses two kinds of nipple, the good nipple and the bad nipple, which ultimately grow into two kinds of mother, the good mother and the bad mother. That is, the mother does not become a simple *personification* until quite late on, and until then there can be more than one personification of the same body. By the same token, no discrimination is made between the tender actual mother and a tender mother's helper.

Sullivan differentiates between the functionally useless and the functionally useful. It is useful to differentiate good mothers and bad mothers, and different responses are made to them, but differential behaviour is not required to a sense of one good mother or another. Only functionally useful stimuli become organized into the infant's experience, Sullivan thinks, once again making a point in accordance with the principles of learning.

Infantile thumb sucking stands in a different relationship to the oral zonal need from feeding, because it invariably produces satisfaction (of the zonal tension, not of hunger tension). No other person is involved in satisfying the zonal need, and the thumb also *feels sucked*.

Sullivan raises two issues over this *self-sentient* aspect of feeling one's own thumb being sucked, in contrast to the *non-self-sentient* characteristic of breast sucking. In the former, Sullivan invests the oral zone with a surplus energy so that sucking behaviour may continue without necessarily involving the hunger need. In other words, because sucking occurs other than for nutritional purposes, an oral dynamism must exist over and above the need for satisfaction of hunger. Thus there are zonal dynamisms in their own right that originate in tension needs. Secondly, and this is more directly concerned with self-sentience, out of the feeling of sucking one's own thumb grows the concept of 'my body' and eventually 'my personality' or as Sullivan puts it, 'the delusion of unique individuality'.[39] That is, although what a person becomes is a result of his interpersonal relationships he has a peculiar relationship with his own body that is missing from his interpersonal contacts, and it is this peculiarity of self-sentience that generates the awareness of a unique me, first of all in a physical, and ultimately in a psychological sense.

When the zonal needs come into operation, the reactions of the mother will be governed by her own social attitudes towards such behaviours as thumb sucking, playing with faeces, fingering the genitals, and so on. Any anxiety that the mother may feel, Sullivan says, induces anxiety in the infant so that a process of what he calls 'long circuiting' of social needs begins. The infant learns to behave in socially acceptable ways, ways that serve to maintain security and minimize anxiety in satisfying its needs. It comes to *sublimate*, to satisfy its needs wholly or partly in ways that do not arouse anxiety in the mother. The success of social training in later infancy depends upon how the mother responds to the infant. Sullivan recommends *consistency*, *frequency*, and *sanity* on the mother's part.

Consistency and frequency are perhaps self-explanatory, but by sanity, or rather insanities, Sullivan refers particularly to some cultural expectations that the mother may have of the infant. One of these is regarding the infant as self-willed, as deliberately engaging in malevolent behaviour when, in fact, whatever the child does depends on her own behaviour towards it. A second unrealistic demand on the infant, according to Sullivan, is that it should be clean and dry by about 15 months of age, and a third is that the infant should be prevented from fondling its genitals.

Parental reactions to these and similar infantile activities vary from place to place and time to time, so the particular examples that Sullivan gives are of limited importance, but his more general contention that parents should recognize their own responsibility for whatever behaviour their infants exhibit is universally valid no matter what society's attitudes may be towards certain infantile habits.

Childhood

The transition from infancy to childhood, both of which are pre-school eras, is marked by the acquisition of language. Not that there are no linguistic signs in the infant; it has acquired cultural gestures and melodic intonations by imitation, but these are 'superstitions' and are not understood in the normal sense or used communicatively. One of the effects of language is to realign functional discriminations that were made in infancy. For example, the word 'Mama' as applied to a particular physical person forces the personification of mother into a single unique object. The good mother and the bad mother become one and the same person (if indeed they are), and the good mother and the good mother's helper are discriminated by name.

The processes begun in infancy continue in childhood, although by now Sullivan considers the self-system to be 'extraordinarily resistant to change by experience'.[40] The self-system (organized through interpersonal activities in infancy that avoided or minimized anxiety, and a network of security operations) resists change even in the face of negative instances. In this respect the self-system network is much more unbending than are satisfaction operations:

> Whereas any recurrent experience will quite soon be added to, and will modify, the manifestations of any dynamism in the satisfaction of needs, the particular structural and functional activity of the self-system is such that a person can go through a whole series of consistent failures of what we call security operations – which is the typical performance when the self-dynamism is the central motor of activity – without learning much of anything. In fact, the chances are that self-system activity will come in *more* readily at the faint hint of anxiety provoking situations, but still without showing the type of profit from failures that would appear in connection with the satisfaction of more biologically conditioned needs.[41]

So, in effect, Sullivan distinguishes between the case of behaviour modifications that are motivated by what experimental psychologists have called *primary drives* and those that are motivated by anxiety or avoidance of noxious consequences. He supposes the latter to be more resistant to extinction, which is in accordance with laboratory evidence.[42]

The resistance to change of the self-system, Sullivan states in his *Theorem of Escape*, which says, in part, that 'the self-system ... tends to escape influence by experience which is incongruous with its current organization and functional activity'.

Another theorem he calls the *Theorem of Reciprocal Emotion*. This is more general than the Theorem of Tenderness, which allows only for the resolution of the complementary needs of mother and infant. The Theorem of Reciprocal Emotion allows for the increased age of the child and the extra demands that the mother makes of it. It recognizes that complementary needs may be aggravated instead of resolved as the child grows up. In full, the extended theorem reads:

> Integration in an interpersonal situation is a reciprocal process in which (1) complementary needs are resolved or aggravated; (2) reciprocal patterns of activity are developed, or disintegrated; and (3) foresight of satisfaction, or rebuff of similar needs is facilitated.[43]

When interaction does not result in mutual need satisfaction the interaction is called *disjunctive* in contrast to a more satisfactory conjunctive, or integrative condition. As the child grows up and is less and less indulged, as it is seen as no longer helpless but able to co-operate, so the possibilities of disjunctive situations increase. Sullivan describes behavioural solutions to security losses in disjunctive situations that are similar to the defence mechanisms postulated by orthodox psychoanalysts. He mentions particularly sublimation, regression, dramatization and preoccupation.

> *Sublimation is the unwitting substitution, for a behaviour pattern which encounters anxiety or collides with the self-system, of a socially more acceptable activity pattern which satisfies part of the motivational system that caused the trouble.*[44]

Sublimated behaviour may be the result of differential anxiety avoidance that takes place without the intervention of conscious decision. But sublimated activity may satisfy only part of a need to reduce anxiety; the remainder of the need could be satisfied either overtly in a socially acceptable manner, or covertly through fantasies and dreams. Regression means returning to an earlier behaviour pattern that had been successful in infancy, and can occur when contemporary behaviour becomes disorganized, either because of aversive consequences or because social control is weakened.

Dramatizations Sullivan also calls 'as if' performances, and these resemble what the Freudians call identification and introjection. That is, as Sullivan says, the child learns to deceive malevolent authorities by *acting-like* and *sounding-like* them and finally playing at *being* them, as in the particular case of identification-with-the-aggressor. Preoccupation, finally, is obsessional engagement in some behaviour that subjectively serves to avoid anxiety, but that is not objectively or logically or causally instrumental in alleviating the unsatisfactory state of affairs. It is irrational behaviour and appears to be functional in the same way as does a superstitious ritual that occasionally coincides with the required result.

In spite of behaviours that may appear to be wrong or malevolent in childhood, Sullivan does not believe that humans are fundamentally evil. Mischief and malevolence in the child, he says, stem out of specific interpersonal occurrences. A typical malevolence-producing relationship is when a child experiences a need for tenderness, but does not get it. Instead, it is treated in a way that provokes anxiety, fear and even pain. In that case, the perceived need for tenderness produces the foresight of anxiety, and the child comes to act as though it is surrounded by enemies. This condition, if it persists into the juvenile era, serves to make it more and more difficult for new associates to remain tender towards the juvenile, and so perpetuates his or her engagement in malevolent relationships.

The juvenile era

The onset of the juvenile period is marked by the beginning of formal education. It is characterized by an apparent need for compeers, for real rather than imaginary friends and playmates. It is the period when the child enters into interpersonal relationships of an enduring nature outside those of the home. It is the period when idiosyncracies of the home environment are exposed and compared to alternative systems of values.

Sullivan's principal concepts about what is happening in the juvenile era are *social subordination* and *social accommodation*, which mean, respectively, that juveniles must subordinate themselves to many more authority figures, particularly teachers, than heretofore, and extend the range of their behaviour to accommodate the activities of other juveniles. The juvenile is able to learn not only from its own direct experiences, from the consequences of its own actions, but also from the example of other juveniles (i.e. peer pressure).

> The juvenile can see what other juveniles are doing – either getting away with, or being reproved for – can notice differences between people which he had never conceived of, because previously he had had nothing whatever on which to base an idea of something different from his own experience.[45]

So, the outstanding characteristic of the juvenile era is an expanding participation in interpersonal relationships, and the child's role in these relationships requires competitive and co-operative behaviours. He or she is no longer solely in a position of dependency upon adults.

The world in which the growing child operates is now immensely more complex than heretofore, and it is this complexity that Sullivan believes is responsible for the so-called latency period. The ideas and operations of childhood are given up, extinguished, because awareness is now focused on the problems of interaction with other juveniles. Their criticism and applause serve to shape experience. Personal concern with one's own body is driven out of focal awareness because of the pressure of other facets of interpersonal living, of co-operating and competing with a group of other juveniles whose values differ from those of the immediate family constellation.

The juvenile phase is the first great correcting era of distortions of awareness engendered in early life and, if things go well, the child should emerge from it *adequately oriented* for future living.

Preadolescence

Emergence into preadolescence is indicated by a constriction of interpersonal activity and by a qualitative addition to the dimensions of interpersonal living. Usually between the ninth and tenth years, Sullivan believes, there develops a need for intimacy. This is exemplified by the formation of small groups of two or three friends. There develops a sensitivity to the needs and requirements of another person, the intimate same-sex chum, where the quality of the relationship between the chums is changed from mere juvenile co-operation to *collaboration*: to a sense of 'we-ness'. That is, in preadolescence another person comes to *matter*, in contrast to juvenile attitudes whereby co-operation or competition are maintained solely in terms of *personal* gain.

This intimate collaborating with a chum provides further and much more intensive opportunity for evaluation of personal worth. One sees oneself for the first time through another's eyes, through eyes that provide for a re-evaluation of any 'fantastic personification of oneself' that may have been maintained during the juvenile era, and that could not have been corrected because the juvenile lacks concern about others. The preadolescent phase enables personal values to be worked out by consensual validation, one chum with the other.

A difficulty that can arise in this era is loneliness, a condition that Sullivan compares in severity with anxiety. In fact, he says: 'Under loneliness, people seek companionship even though intensely anxious in the performance.'[46] Not that loneliness is peculiar to preadolescence – it has its origin at least as early as childhood – but it is in this era that it is most acutely felt because of the intensity of the need for intimacy in the companionship of a chum.

Sullivan does not believe that the roots of personality are sunk only in early childhood, or that the patterns of later behaviour are thereafter established and immutable. It is true that he frequently refers to the early stabilization of the self-system, and to its resistance to change by negative instances, but he also acknowledges that it is open to change when circumstances are powerful enough to warrant it. And in preadolescence there are powerful forces – loneliness is one of them – and there are also novel circumstances, of which the interpersonal quality of collaboration is perhaps the most important.

Early adolescence

Unlike Freud, Sullivan does not treat infantile sexuality in the same way as mature genital sexuality. He regards entry into early adolescence as the first awakening of genital interest, which he describes as *lust*. In this era, the need for intimacy is said to change its object from collaboration with one of the same sex – what

Sullivan calls an *isophilic choice*, seeking someone like oneself – to one of the other sex, a *heterophilic choice* of someone unlike oneself, genitalia-wise.

Because of individual differences in age of puberty, there are particular interpersonal difficulties involved in the transition from pre– to early adolescence. Chums, for example, who collaborate in satisfying each other's intimacy needs when isophilic choices are appropriate before puberty, can no longer do so when a heterophilic choice is determined by the lustful needs of one or the other of them. Security operations that were successful during preadolescence, are now threatened by the lust dynamism. There are opportunities for collisions between the intimacy need and lust while the intimacy need is still tied to an isophilic choice, for collisions between a new object of the intimacy need and the maintenance of security, and for collisions between the need for security and lust.

The pre-adolescent isophilic choices, Sullivan says, are useful in preparing the individual for forthcoming relationships with his or her own sex in adulthood, but they do nothing to prepare either sex for genital exploration in early adolescence. And it is here that security is threatened when initial sexual advances are clumsy and unsatisfactory in their outcome, and when an *autophilic* choice of masturbation engenders anxiety and guilt.

Storms and stresses of adolescence are the result of cultural practices. One particularly pernicious possible outcome that Sullivan singles out is the characterization of females into good girls and bad girls – the good girls for the alleviation of loneliness and the bad girls for the satisfaction of lust. This can lead to all sorts of troubles in maturity when love and lust are permissible with only one person, who may be quite unprepared for one or the other role.

Late adolescence

Sullivan distinguishes between early and late adolescence on the grounds of *achievement*, not biological maturity. Biologically, persons are already sexually mature in early adolescence but their sexuality is not an integral part of the rest of their living: 'A person begins late adolescence when he discovers what he likes in the way of genital behaviour and how to fit it into the rest of life.'[47] From here on, if the opportunities occur and if early preparation has been adequate, the individual enters maturity.

Through all these eras it is well to remember that Sullivan is not talking about a biologically developing organism. Biological development is occurring, of course, but Sullivan is offering a classification of kinds of interpersonal contacts that become important as a person grows older and moves into different positions in the community. These are the interpersonal situations that Sullivan considers to be important for the formation of adult behaviour patterns. In these accounts of typical examples of everyday living, Sullivan engages in descriptions of human personality that transcend the laboratory boundaries of the functional behaviourists. But his speculations about how these behaviour patterns can come about are remarkably harmonious with the principles of operant psychology.

Part II

Behavioural Mechanics

4

Respondent Conditioning: Pavlov

The dynamics of behaviour that I have described so far derive mostly from clinical observations of human psychiatric patients. These accounts naturally revolve around conceptions of the nature of personality as an individual particularity. When it comes to testing theories of behaviour in general, animals are frequently employed as replacement models for humans, and instead of the nature of personality occupying centre-stage the spotlight focuses on the stimulus control of particular responses.

The first systematic investigations into the stimulus control of behaviour were initiated by the Russian physiologist Ivan Pavlov. The most elementary way of controlling behaviour is by the elicitation of a reflex. Reflexes are automatic responses to certain natural stimuli: when a stimulus is presented the appropriate response is evoked. Common examples are the knee-jerk when the patellar tendon is tapped, pupillary constriction when a light is shone in the eye, blinking when the eyeball is irritated, changes in heart rate and blood distribution in response to startling or painful events.

Although they are numerous, reflexes nonetheless form only a small part of the behavioural repertoire of higher organisms, and behavioural control by means of the natural stimuli that elicit reflexes is limited to a relatively few simple acts. However, reflexes are sometimes evoked by non-natural stimuli. Salivation occurs as a reflex to the natural stimulus of food in the mouth, but the sight and smell of food may also evoke salivation. This fact was known and studied at least as early as the eighteenth century, and can be observed by anyone who feeds a pet dog at the table. One of the earliest references to what has since come to be called classical, or respondent, conditioning was made by the English philosopher David Hartley who, in 1749, wrote in his *Observations on Man*:

> The fingers of young children bend upon almost every impression which is made upon the palm of the hand, thus performing the act of grasping, in the original automatic manner. After a sufficient repetition of the motor vibrations which occur in this action ... associated with other vibrations ... the most common of which, I suppose, are those excited by a favourite plaything which the child used to grasp ... he ought, therefore, according to the doctrine of association to perform and repeat the action of grasping, upon having such a plaything presented to his sight. But it is a known fact that children do this.

I have omitted Hartley's archaic neurological terminology, but the impact of his remarks is in the last sentence. Over two hundred years ago the elicitation of a reflex by an unnatural stimulus was 'a known fact', and Hartley ventures an opinion on how this fact comes about – by the repeated association of the natural and the unnatural stimuli.

Like so many things scientific, the fact of conditioning was known long before its systematic investigation, and the importance of this investigation turned out to be in a field quite different from that which its author intended.[1] George Bernard Shaw, through the medium of the little black girl in his play *The Adventures of the Black Girl in her Search of God*, illustrates a common attitude towards the first point. He also demonstrates his contempt for the researches of Pavlov. In the passage below, the myopic old man is Pavlov himself. The little black girl has run away from one of her earlier gods.

> 'What am I running away from?' she said to herself, pulling herself up. 'I'm not afraid of that dear noisy old man.'
> 'Your fears and hopes are only fancies' said a voice close to her, proceeding from a very shortsighted elderly man in spectacles who was sitting on a gnarled log. 'In running away you were acting on a conditioned reflex. It is quite simple. Having lived among lions you have from your childhood associated the sound of a roar with deadly danger. Hence your precipitate flight when that superstitious old jackass brayed at you. This remarkable discovery cost me twenty-five years of devoted research, during which I cut out the brains of

innumerable dogs, and observed their spittle by making holes in their cheeks for them to salivate through instead of through their tongues. The whole scientific world is prostrate at my feet in admiration of this colossal achievement and gratitude for the light it has shed on the great problems of human conduct.'

'Why didn't you ask me?' said the black girl, 'I could have told you in twenty-five seconds without hurting those poor dogs.'

As it happens, Pavlov did not discover the fact of conditioning 'after twenty-five years of devoted research', He began with the fact and devoted a quarter of a century and more in teasing out its details and ramifications. In twenty-five seconds he too could have told as much as the little black girl without hurting any poor dogs. In fact Shaw has him say so:

'Your ignorance and presumption are unspeakable' said the old myop. The fact was known of course to every child; but it had never been proved experimentally in the laboratory; and therefore it was not scientifically known at all. It reached me as an unskilled conjecture: I handed it on as science. Have you ever performed an experiment, may I ask?'[2]

The little black girl answered the old man's question in the affirmative and proceeded to perform an experiment which left him clinging for his life to the limb of a tree.

'How am I to come down?' said the myop trembling, 'I should break my neck.'

'How did you get up?' said the black girl.

'I don't know,' he replied, almost in tears, 'It is enough to make a man believe in miracles. I couldn't have climbed this tree; and yet here I am and shall never be able to get down again.'

'A very interesting experiment, wasn't it?' said the black girl.

'A shamefully cruel one, you wicked girl' he moaned. 'Pray did it occur to you that you might have killed me? Do you suppose you can give a delicate physiological organism like mine a violent shock without the most serious and quite possibly fatal reactions on the heart? I shall never be able to sit on a log again as long as I live. I believe my pulse is quite abnormal, though I cannot count it; for if I let go of this branch I shall drop like a stone.'

'If you can cut half a dog's brain out without causing any reactions on its spittle you need not worry' she said calmly. 'I think African magic much more powerful than your divining by dogs. By saying one word to you I made you climb a tree like a cat. You confess it was a miracle.'

'I wish you would say another word and get me safely down again, confound you for a black witch' he grumbled.

'I will,' said the black girl. 'There is a tree snake smelling at the back of your neck.'

The myop was on the ground in a jiffy. He landed finally on his back; but he scrambled to his feet at once and said 'You did not take me in: don't think it. I knew perfectly well you were inventing that snake to frighten me.'

'And yet you were as frightened as if it had been a real snake,' said the black girl.

'I was not,' said the myop indignantly. 'I was not frightened in the least.'[3]

The little black girl's experiment was not the first imaginative one of its kind. A letter from W.A. Bousfield printed in the *American Psychologist* in December 1955 contains the following translation of a passage by Lope de Vega written in the seventeenth century.

Saint Ildefonso used to scold me and punish me lots of times. He would sit me on the bare floor and make me eat with the cats of the monastery. These cats were such rascals that they took advantage of my penitence. They drove me mad stealing my choicest morsels. It did no good to chase them away. But I found a way of coping with the beasts in order to enjoy my meals when I was punished. I put them all in a sack, and on a pitch black night took them out under an arch. First I would cough and then immediately whale the daylights out of the cats. They whined and shrieked like an infernal pipe organ. I would pause for awhile and repeat the operation – first a cough, and then a thrashing. I finally noticed that even without beating them, the beasts moaned and yelped like the very devil whenever I coughed. I let them loose. Thereafter, whenever I had to eat off the floor, I would cast a look around. If an animal approached my food, all I had to do was to cough, and how that cat did scat!

Before giving his attention to the systematic study of conditioning, Pavlov was already a physiologist of renown through his studies of the digestive processes in dogs. It was through the eyes of a physiologist that he viewed his work, which he saw as applying not to the behaviour of an organism, but to the analysis of its nervous and cortical activity. He did not at first see himself as contributing to the science of psychology; in fact he did not think of psychology as a science at all, and quoted Wundt and William James, the most eminent psychologists of his day, to that effect.

Pavlov began his research on conditioning as the 19th century was coming to an end, and of his beginning he was quite explicit:

> In the course of a detailed investigation into the activities of the digestive glands I had to inquire into the so-called psychic secretion of some of the glands, a task which I attempted in conjunction with a collaborator. As a result of this investigation an unqualified conviction of the futility of subjective methods of inquiry was firmly stamped upon my mind. It became clear that the only satisfactory solution of the problem lay in an experimental investigation by strictly objective methods. For this purpose I started to record all the external stimuli falling on the animal at the time its reflex reaction was manifested (in this particular case the secretion of saliva), at the same time recording all changes in the reaction of the animal.[4]

Pavlov never did live up to this high ideal. He succeeded in having a laboratory built so that, as far as possible, he could reduce and control the external stimulation to which his subjects were exposed. But he limited his systematic observations only to certain kinds of behaviour – natural reflexes – usually salivation to food or acid in the mouth:

> It is essential to realize that each of these two reflexes – the alimentary reflex and the mild defence reflex to rejectable substances – consists of two distinct components, a motor and a secretory. Firstly the animal exhibits a reflex activity directed towards getting hold of the food and eating it or, in the case of rejectable substances, towards getting rid of them out of the mouth; and secondly, in both cases an immediate secretion of saliva occurs, in the case of food, to start the physical and chemical processes of digestion and, in the case of rejectable substances, to wash them out of the mouth. We confined our experiments almost entirely to the secretory component of the reflex: the allied motor reactions were taken into account only where there were special reasons. The secretory reflex presents many important advantages for our purpose. It allows of an extremely accurate measurement of the intensity of reflex activity, since either the number of drops in a given time may be counted or else the saliva may be caused to displace a coloured fluid in a horizontally placed

graduated glass tube. It would be much more difficult to obtain the same accuracy of measurement for any motor reflex, especially for such complex motor reactions as accompany reflexes to food or to rejectable substances.[5]

So Pavlov knew that food and acid in the mouth evoked motor as well as secretory reflexes but confined himself to the secretory component except where special conditions required the motor reactions to be taken into account. It was with this decision that the scientific, objective study of conditioning began.

The foundations of conditioning

The classical method of establishing a conditioned reflex is as follows. By means of the surgical operation that upset Bernard Shaw, Pavlov exposed the salivary duct of a dog. Over it he cemented a small funnel for collecting saliva at feeding times. When it is hungry, the dog is taken to a familiar room where it is harnessed to the recording equipment. Meanwhile, the experimenter observes the dog and records its reactions from an adjoining cubicle.

Typically, a metronome is occasionally set beating for a few seconds. After a brief prick of the ears (investigatory reflex), the dog remains more or less indifferent. Two or three such trials serve to establish that the dog does not salivate naturally to the sound. After this, a little powdered meat drops into a pan under the animal's nose whenever the beating resumes. The dog does not respond to the metronome alone, but salivates when it eats the food. Again and again the metronome sounds and the food is given, and every time the animal takes the food and salivates. Before long a few drops of saliva are recorded *before* the food is presented, and very quickly the animal comes to salivate as copiously to the beating metronome as it once did to the food alone. We can now talk of a *conditioned reflex*; the reflex of salivation, natural to the food stimulus, is elicited by the sound of the beating metronome. Salivation has now become a conditioned reflex (CR) and the metronome a conditioned stimulus (CS). The food is called an *unconditioned stimulus* (US), and its function, which at the beginning was to *elicit* salivation as an *unconditioned reflex* (UR), is now to *reinforce* the eliciting powers of the CS. The only condition necessary for the acquisition of these powers by the CS is that it signals when food is forthcoming.[6]

Pavlov viewed the brain and nervous system as a telephone exchange. Messages come in, pass through the central exchange, and are relayed out. In the case of reflexes, the central exchange is eliminated and replaced, as it were, by a direct line. The process of conditioning amounts to the laying of a new direct line in the brain, *from the cortical centre associated with the CS to the centre associated with the US*. Now, when CS and US are presented together, the neural activity set off by the CS is drawn to the centre excited by the US. As excitation of the US centre is directly connected to the UR centre, the neural activity from the CS passes on to elicit the CR. But at first, this extra excitation from the CS centre is weak and so requires reinforcement by excitatory processes set in motion by the US, just as an army doing battle requires reinforcement before the initial impetus of its ferocity dies out. Continued passage of the reinforced excitatory processes serves to establish the neural pathway between the CS and US centres more and more firmly, so that eventually the excitation process set off by the CS makes its way to the UR centre in sufficient strength to evoke the response unaided.

This simple view of conditioning was greatly complicated as a result of Pavlov's later work, but it serves to show how he meant the term reinforcement to be understood. It was only through reinforcement that the CS could come to elicit the CR, and this, to Pavlov, indicated that an association between CS and US had been formed.[7]

Acquisition and extinction

Pavlov and Freud were contemporaries and they were both influenced by the associationistic mental philosophy of their era. Freud, as we saw, focused on association of ideas by their significance to the individual; Pavlov studied the association of stimuli and responses according to the time interval between them.

Figure 4.1 depicts the event of conditioning. The upper three horizontal lines indicate the presence or absence of the CS, US and response respectively, a displacement upwards marking onset and downwards showing offset of the variable in question. The lower line marks the passage of time. Thus, in Figure 4.1A, the CS occurs

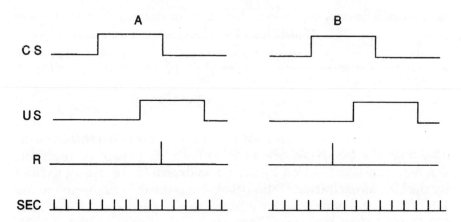

Figure 4.1. Simultaneous conditioning. The upper three lines represent onset (displacement upwards) and offset (displacement downwards) of the conditioned (CS) and unconditioned (US) stimuli, and the occurrence of the response (R). The bottom line is the time scale. A shows the natural reflex before conditioning; B is after conditioning. In this case, R precedes the US, which now becomes the reinforcer.

but produces no response, as is shown by the fact that R coincides with US onset. The state of affairs *after* repeated pairing of CS and US is shown in Figure 4.1B. The response now *precedes* the US and occurs to the CS alone. The time between the beginning of the CS and the appearance of the CR is known as the *latency* of the CR and is one measure of CR strength.

Were other diagrams included to show the state of affairs between Figures 4.1A and 4.1B it would be seen that when the CS-US interval is kept brief, the CR latency gradually decreases: the appearance of the CR slowly moves forward in the sequence of events. In the same way the onset of the CR would be seen to be gradual, occurring more and more frequently and in greater and greater amount on successive blocks of trials. Frequency and amount (magnitude) are other measures of CR strength.

When CS precedes US by only a short time, conditioning is rapid and strong. The technique is known as simultaneous conditioning, but if the US precedes the CS by an equally brief interval (a procedure known as backward conditioning) the CS does not acquire the same power to elicit a reflex. Two other temporal relationships that Pavlov studied are delayed and trace conditioning. In both cases, the onset of the US may occur a minute or more after the CS is turned on. The procedures are different because in delayed conditioning the two stimuli overlap, whereas in the trace procedure the CS is terminated before US onset. In this case CS and US are not contiguous at all.

The observations that contiguity can occur without conditioning (backward conditioning), and that conditioning can occur without contiguity (trace conditioning), suggests that more than contiguity is involved in the conditioning process.

The speed with which trace and delayed conditioned reflexes are formed depends upon a number of variables, including the amount of pre-training given with the short delay procedures, the kind of CS used and the sense modality to which it is applied. Also important is what Pavlov calls the temperament of the experimental animal:

> In some dogs the establishment of the reflex is rapid while in others the beginning of the salivary secretion persistently refuses to separate itself from the beginning of the conditioned stimulus, and the development of delay is very slow.[8]

Pavlov appeals to a process of inhibition (see below) to account for trace and delayed reflexes. On a number of occasions when investigating the nature of this process, he ran into wide differences in the ways his dogs behaved. On the basis of this he ventured a rudimentary theory on the relation of personality and conditioning, a theory that has since been systematized and amplified by groups led by Teplov in Russia and Eysenck in Britain.[9]

A more elaborate form of conditioning is *higher order conditioning*. This is a particularly important form of conditioning because it provides for the transference of control from one initially neutral stimulus to another, so that the CR may come under the control of a CS that has never been paired directly with the US. An illustration of second order conditioning is shown in Figure 4.2.

In the first stage, a normal CR is established to a CS1, a bell for example, using the usual US of food to reinforce the action of the bell. At the second stage, a new stimulus, CS2, a black square, say, is paired with the bell by the usual simultaneous conditioning procedure. At first, the CS1 alone evokes the CR because of its

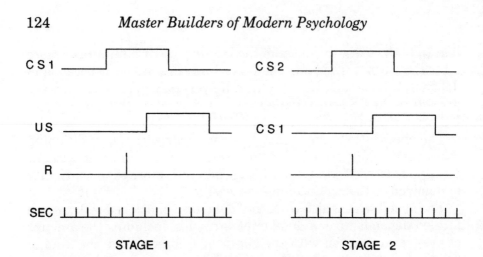

CS1   CS2

US   CS1

R

SEC

STAGE 1   STAGE 2

Figure 4.2. Higher order conditioning. At first, the response is conditioned to CS1 (Stage 1, see Figure 4.1), then this stimulus is used to reinforce the conditioned response to CS2.

pairing with the US in Stage 1, but eventually the CR may be made to the new stimulus, CS2. The original CS1 now exhibits the power to reinforce the effects of CS2 in addition to its acquired elicitation properties, and is called a *secondary reinforcer*.[10] During Stage 2, the CS1 is no longer reinforced (followed by the US) and it loses its properties both as a CS and as a reinforcer, so that unless special care is taken, instead of higher order conditioning, *extinction* results.

Conditioned responses do not decay spontaneously with time; they must be removed by a technique that Pavlov called *experimental extinction*. When a CS is presented alone, that is, not reinforced by the US, the CR weakens and finally disappears. Because extinction does not occur spontaneously, Pavlov believed that the weakening of a CR came about not by a direct reduction in its own strength but by the growth of an opposing neural process of *inhibition*, the opposite of *excitation*, which he believed occurred in the establishment of a CR.

Pavlov used the concept of inhibition to account for a number of experimental phenomena that he observed. In the first place, he assumed that inhibition was responsible for the delayed appearance of CRs in trace and delayed conditioning. He supported this assumption by demonstrating that a novel stimulus introduced during the delay period evoked the CR immediately. This he called *disinhibition*. On the other hand, a novel stimulus introduced during the excitatory phase of simultaneous conditioning inhibits the CR. These observations are consistent if a novel stimulus opposes an ongoing process – excitation in the case of simultaneous conditioning and inhibition during the CS-US interval in trace and delayed conditioning.

Another important consideration for the two-process theory is the course of extinction. If a series of extinction trials follow one after the other, a more or less orderly decrease in CR strength occurs. But if there is a gap between blocks of extinction trials, the CR recovers part of its strength in the interval: CR strength is greater at the beginning of the second (extinction) session than it was at the end of the first. Pavlov called this *spontaneous recovery*, and explained it by reference to the spontaneous decay of inhibition. That is, during extinction, he said, inhibition builds up in opposition to the excitatory strength of the CR, and so weakens the manifestation of the reflex. In rest periods the inhibition is supposed to decay, so that the net excitatory strength is higher by the beginning of the next set of trials. The explanation is appealing for its ingenuity, but it is disingenuous to account for spontaneous recovery of excitation as spontaneous decay of inhibition.

Generalization and discrimination

When a response is conditioned to a particular stimulus, a tone of 1,000 Hertz, say, it is also evoked by higher and lower tones, but with less magnitude. Responses conditioned to one stimulus generalize to other stimuli, the amount of generalization corresponding to the degree of similarity between the stimuli. The counterpart of generalization from one stimulus to another is *discrimination* between stimuli. When a CR established to one stimulus generalizes to other stimuli the 'band-width', or spread, of the generalization gradient is not affected by continued training with the original CS only. Generalization can only be reduced, or discrimination sharpened, by differential reinforcement. While the original CS is reinforced, reinforcement is withheld when the to-be-discriminated stimulus (technically, the differential stimulus) occurs. In this way, the CR can be made more and more specific to a single CS as the conditioned and differential stimuli are made more and more alike.

There is a limit to discrimination. One of Pavlov's associates conditioned a dog to salivate to a circle but not to an ellipse: responses to the circle were reinforced but those to the ellipse were not. At first there was generalization to the ellipse but soon a discrimination was formed. Then gradually more and more circular ellipses were presented unreinforced among reinforced exposures to the circle. As Pavlov describes it,

> The differentiation proceeded with some fluctuations, progressing at first more and more quickly, and then again slower, until an ellipse with ratio of semiaxes 9:8 was reached ... After three weeks of work upon this differentiation not only did the discrimination fail to improve, but it became considerably worse, and finally disappeared altogether ... The hitherto quiet dog began to squeal in its stand, kept wriggling about, tore off ... apparatus ... and bit through the tubes ...; in short it presented all the symptoms of acute neurosis.[11]

This is an example of *experimental neurosis* and was explained by Pavlov as a clash between excitatory and inhibitory activities in the cerebral cortex.

It was the workings of the brain that Pavlov sought to unravel by his studies on conditioning, not the phenomena of learning. He used the conditioned response as a medium for making inferences about the brain and although his technical terminology – excitation, inhibition, extinction, spontaneous recovery, reinforcement, and the rest – have been incorporated into the lexicon of the psychology of learning, it was the analysis of cortical functioning in terms of excitation and inhibition that occupied the greater part of Pavlov's experimental ingenuity.

The result that he arrived at concerning the effects of brain stimulation can be compared to the effects of dropping a pebble into a pool of water. According to Pavlov's interpretation of his studies of conditioning, when a brain centre is stimulated a phase of excitation spreads out across the cortex from this point. At the same time, this spread of excitation leaves behind a temporary state of inhibition. Eventually, the excitatory wave rebounds and concentrates back to its point of origin, interacting on the way with the inhibitory state that it originally induced. This is a long way from Pavlov's beginning:

> Our starting point has been Descartes' idea of the nervous reflex. This is a genuine scientific conception, since it implies necessity. It may be summed up as follows: an external or internal stimulus falls on some one or other nervous receptor and gives rise to a nervous impulse; this nervous impulse is transmitted along nerve fibres to the central nervous system, and here, on account of existing nervous connections, it gives rise to a fresh impulse which passes along outgoing nerve fibres to the active organ, where it excites a special activity of the cellular process. *Thus a stimulus appears to be connected of necessity with a definite response, as cause with effect.*[12]

This mechanical type of nervous system must also, he argues, be adaptive: 'if, instead of being attracted to food the animal were repelled by it, or if instead of running from fire the animal threw itself into the fire, then it would quickly perish.' But survival requires more than this:

> The strong carnivorous animal preys on weaker animals, and these if they waited to defend themselves until the teeth of the foe were in their flesh would speedily be exterminated. The case takes on a different aspect when the defence reflex is called into play by the sights and sounds of the enemy's approach. Then the prey has a chance to save itself by hiding or by flight.[13]

If the mechanical, natural, stimulus for the defence reflex is the actuality of fangs in the flesh then the reflex defence reaction would be too late for the prey to survive. Some means of transferring the stimulus control of defence from the teeth to the sights and sounds of the enemy are required, and the techniques of conditioning that Pavlov used help to serve this end.

Parametric and conceptual elaborations

Pavlov began the systematic study of respondent conditioning and provided the technical terminology that has since been extended to the psychology of learning. Pavlov discovered numerous phenomena of a qualitative nature that he pursued quantitatively for the information they might give about the workings of the brain, and the same kind of tradition has been followed by his Russian successors. American workers, on the other hand, have concentrated on the quantitative, parametric, aspects of conditioning.

There are several variables involved in the respondent conditioning paradigm: the unconditioned response, the unconditioned stimulus, the conditioned stimulus and the experimental organism. Pavlov had something to contribute to each of these aspects of conditioning, but there have been important conceptual elaborations in every one of them by more modern psychologists.

The unconditioned response

The essential feature of conditioning is the conditioned response: whether it occurs, when it occurs and how long it lasts. This is so whether we are interested in the response as an instance of behaviour that is learned or whether we see it as an objective indication of processes presumed to be occurring in the brain. Pavlov worked extensively with the secretion of saliva as the unconditioned response, chiefly because his work evolved from his interest in the process of digestion. In this sense, the use of salivation as the reflex to be conditioned is probably more an accident of history than a result of scientific considerations, although Pavlov explicitly chose to study salivation over movement for ease of quantification, as noted above. But leg flexion elicited by electric shock was also studied in Pavlov's laboratory.

Since the beginning, conditioning of a wide variety of natural reflexes has been claimed, including the pupillary reflex, nausea and vomiting, various vasomotor reactions, changes in skin resistance, the patellar reflex, sucking, the Babkin reflex (mouth opening in newborn infants when the palms of the hands are pressed simultaneously while the infant is supine), eye movements, heart rate and respiration changes, eyeblinking and so on. Various instructed responses, such as squeezing a bulb and tapping a Morse key, have also been included in the category of classically conditioned responses. However, these are not reflexive responses no matter how automatic they may become, and if we are to maintain the naturally evoked reflex as the cornerstone of the Pavlovian paradigm these and other apparent examples of conditioned behaviour must be reassessed.

Conditioned and unconditioned responses need not be identical, which would not be possible if conditioning is merely the transfer of control of a reflex from one eliciting stimulus to another. When differences between conditioned and unconditioned responses occur, they could be the result of the addition of instrumental behaviours to the conditioned response complex or to significant changes in the characteristics of the unconditioned response itself caused by the Pavlovian procedure.[14]

It is not always easy to identify a conditioned response because some reflexes can resemble voluntary behaviour. A good example is eyeblinking. In this case, a puff of air on the cornea elicits a quick blink, which can be conditioned to a light or sound, but there are problems in deciding whether the blinks are truly conditioned or whether they are voluntary blinks made to avoid discomfort from the puff. A similar situation exists in the case of conditioned leg flexion to electric shock.[15] Whenever a response can occur either voluntarily or involuntarily, the contribution of Pavlovian conditioning to the outcome of the experiment is likely to be in doubt.

Response strength

Conditioned response strength can be measured in several ways. With increasing numbers of CS-US pairings, the CR is said to gain in strength, and this strength is assessed according to the latency and magnitude of the CR. As the CS is evoked more frequently by the CS in later than in earlier blocks of trials, frequency is also employed as a measure of CR strength. Finally strength sometimes is reported in terms of resistance to extinction – the number of unreinforced trials required to extinguish the CR. Unfortunately, these measures do not always give the same result. If frequency and magnitude both increase with training, then they should correlate perfectly and positively (+1.00) with each other if they are alternative measures of response strength. Likewise latency, which decreases with training, should correlate perfectly and negatively (−1.00) with frequency and magnitude.

Allowing for less than perfect reliabilities of the measures, the correlations between amplitude and frequency are reasonable but by no means good.[16] Latency has very little in common with the other indices of reflex strength, although the correlations at least are in the expected direction. A clue to the unreliability of latency as a measure of strength may be in Pavlov's findings with delayed and trace conditioning. The CR does not appear to be tied to the onset of the CS as much as to the presentation of the US. There is no reason, then, to expect a quicker and quicker response to the CS as training proceeds. It might be more reasonable to explore the CR-US interval instead of the CS-CR latency, and some work on eyelid conditioning by Kimmel[17] confirms Pavlov in showing that the CR-US interval becomes shorter and shorter as training progresses.

Resistance to extinction has a complex relationship with CR strength. If all trials are reinforced, then in general, the greater number of trials the harder it is to extinguish the CR. But when only a proportion of the CS presentations are reinforced, extinction is slower than when reinforcement occurs on every trial. As CR magnitude is typically greater with 100 per cent than with partial reinforcement (in fact Pavlov failed to condition a dog reinforced on every fourth trial), resistance to extinction and CR magnitude may be negatively instead of positively correlated. The technique of partial reinforcement as such, and the manner in which reinforcers are scheduled, have been important for respondent and operant conditioning alike, and the question will be explored further in terms of reinforcement schedules in operant conditioning.

Paradoxically, investigations of conditioning may proceed profitably by neglecting the CR altogether.[18] This approach pits respondently conditioned behaviour against ongoing operant behaviour (see Chapter 5), and strength of conditioning is assessed according to the degree of suppression of the operant. The phenomenon is known as the *conditioned emotional reaction* (CER) or conditioned suppression, and was first used as a way of objectively defining anxiety.[19]

The basic procedure involves training an animal to press a lever for occasional reinforcement by food. Once lever pressing is well established, a signal is presented for 3-4 minutes followed by a brief electric shock. At first, the animal ignores the signal, but after a few pairings with shock, the signal elicits competing behaviour to lever pressing, causing the rate of this response to drop when the signal is on. Even though the CRs may never be identified in this case, the eliciting power of the once neutral signal may be assessed by its suppressing effect on other behaviour.[20]

The unconditioned stimulus

The first function of the US is to elicit the UR. To do this, the US must occur with some *intensity*, where intensity is the technical term for the strength of the stimulus: loudness, brightness, force, and so on. Units of stimulus intensity will, of course, vary according to the sense modality stimulated, but a rough comparison across modalities is possible through the psychological concept of *threshold*. The threshold is the intensity level of the US sufficient to elicit a detectable UR. Comparisons between different stimulus-response combinations may therefore be made by equating stimuli by reference to threshold levels even though their physical units of measurement may be quite different.

The second function of the US is to reinforce the operation of the CS once an anticipatory response has come about. In both its eliciting and reinforcing functions, US intensity is an important variable: in the first place a more intense US evokes a UR of greater magnitude, and in the second place a more intense US is a more potent reinforcer than a less intense one. This Pavlov calls the *Law of Intensity*, a law that breaks down in cases of experimental neurosis.[21]

Unconditioned stimuli can be classified as positive, negative or neutral. A positive stimulus is something beneficial, such as food, a negative stimulus is something harmful, such as electric shock, and a neutral stimulus is neither one nor the other, such as a tap on the patellar tendon or a very weak air puff on the eyeball. Pavlov's use of salivation as a UR has a particularly happy choice in this respect, for it is elicited by both positive (Type A, food as US) and negative (Type B, acid as US) stimuli.[22]

A fundamental difference between the types is that extranaeous motivation must be used in Type A but not Type B. Thus, when a positive US (food) is used, it is necessary for the subject to consume it. So the animal must be motivated by food deprivation before experimental proceedings can begin. Pavlov wrote about this:

> In the hungry animal food naturally brings about a powerful uncon-
> ditioned reflex, and the conditioned reflex develops quickly. But in a
> dog which has not long been fed the unconditioned stimulus has only
> a small effect, and alimentary conditioned reflexes either are not
> formed at all or are established very slowly.[23]

Food-depriving the dog makes it more likely to salivate to food
when it is offered, and it also makes it more likely that the food will
be sought and eaten, which adds an instrumental complexity to the
simple respondent of salivation. No such complexity arises when
negative USs are employed. Acid squirted into the mouth elicits
salivation, and electric shock elicits several unconditioned respon-
dents. No extraneous motivation is necessary in Type B
conditioning. Nevertheless, complicating activities do occur, like
squealing, struggling and reluctance to enter the experimental
chamber. Much of this behaviour may drop out (habituate) if it
serves no purpose, but sometimes it persists in the form of experimental neurosis.[24]

An impressive extension of the range of unconditioned stimuli
and their associated responses has been studied by Russian workers.[25] Early demonstrations of conditioning were of reflexes elicited
by exteroceptive stimuli – stimuli that excite sense receptors near
the surface of the body. There are, however, interoceptive receptors
buried in the muscles, viscera and other internal organs that also
elicit reflexive responses. The change in breathing rhythm elicited
when carbon dioxide is inhaled is an example of this kind of reflex.
It has been conditioned to exteroceptive stimuli, like a bell, or to
other interoceptive stimuli. In one case rhythmic distention of an
externalized intestinal loop (interoceptive CS) came to elicit the
hypercapnic respiratory change (interoceptive CR) originally elicited by the mixture of carbon dioxide and air (interoceptive US).
This example of interoceptive-interoceptive conditioning (in contrast to the exteroceptive-exteroceptive type originally studied by
Pavlov) is important theoretically for the light it sheds on unconscious process (because we are not normally conscious of the
internal workings of our bodies) and practically because of its
potential contribution to the provenance and relief of psychosomatic
disorders.

The conditioned stimulus

Numerous conditioned stimuli including metronomes, bubbling water, lights of various colours, buzzers, horns, papers, geometrical forms and various thermal, tactile, and proprioceptive stimuli were employed in Pavlov's laboratory.[26] Reflexes have been conditioned to the onset of stimuli, their termination, as well as to changes in intensity of a conditioned stimulus. Even electric shock has been successfully used as a CS. If interest is centered on the conditions for establishing a CR, then choice of CS may be only a matter of technical convenience, but there are occasions when experimental tactics dictate the choice of one kind of CS over another. For example, lights and sounds can only stimulate the subject in the relatively small anatomical locations of the eye and the ear, whereas tactile and thermal stimuli may be applied anywhere on the body's surface. These latter stimuli are useful for studying *irradiation*.

By irradiation, Pavlov meant the spreading of either excitatory or inhibitory process across the cortex from the place of *primary stimulation* to places of *secondary stimulation*. These terms were particularly used in the case of inhibition, but are equally applicable to the presumed spread of excitation. Table 4.1 shows the results of an experiment that supposedly exhibit the effects of irradiated inhibition. Conditioned salivary reflexes were established to stimulation of seven points on the skin: between the neck

Table 4.1. Evidence given for irradiation of inhibition from the place of primary stimulation to places of secondary stimulation.

Place stimulated	Percentage of inhibition observed at different intervals of time in seconds						
	0	15	30	45	60	120	180
2	30		54		29	19	10
1	45		66		39	22	13
0	91		75		50	37	17
3	52	58	69	57	45	34	13
4	37		65		39	22	13
5	27		57		23	17	11
6	19	26	31	22	20	10	7

From I.P. Pavlov, *Conditioned Reflexes*, 163.

and chest (0), left forelimb (1), left paw (2), middle of the chest (3), pelvis (4), left hind thigh (5), and left hind paw (6).

The response to stimulation at point 0 was then inhibited by pairing the tactile CS with the sound of a buzzer and withholding reinforcement.[27] The cortical projection of this point thus becomes the place of primary extinction, and the cortical projection of the other points are the places of secondary extinction. On the surface of the skin these places are separated from the place of primary extinction in the order of increasing distance 3, 1, 4, 2, 5, 6, and their cortical projections are presumed to follow a similar spatial distribution. If inhibition irradiates across the brain, then the effects of inhibition at any point in time might be expected to be less at points further from the place of primary stimulation than at points closer to it. This is what the data in the table show. They also show that irradiation of inhibition is a function of time. At all of the secondary places, inhibition builds up to a maximum in about thirty seconds, and then begins to decay.

The technicalities of an experiment such as this are quite complex. I cite it not as proof of Pavlov's theories of cortical functions but as an illustration of research possibilities with tactile stimuli that are not possible with the more commonly used visual and auditory stimuli.

Visual and auditory stimuli, however, are more convenient for research on the effect of CS intensity on conditioning. Pavlov himself believed that there is an optimum CS intensity for conditioning. He found conditioned responses difficult to establish to weak (near to threshold) stimuli and also to those that are very strong. To Pavlov's mind, a protecting inhibition develops in the cortex whenever it is assailed by stimuli of sufficient intensity to cause it damage. He noted two peculiarities in conditioning that followed intense cortical stimulation. The first he called the *paradoxical phase*, referring to those occasions when weak CSs would elicit CRs while stronger ones would not. The second he called the *ultraparadoxical phase*, a phase in which *inhibitory* CSs would evoke CRs while normal excitatory ones would not. This peculiar effect he accounted for in terms of *induction*, a phenomenon referring to a temporary state of excitation induced by an inhibitory stimulus, and *vice versa*.

Verbal stimuli: the second signalling system

Thermal and tactile stimuli are useful for studying spatial effects in conditioning, and auditory and visual stimuli are suitable when the effects of intensity are investigated. Another range of phenomena can be explored when *words* are used as conditioned stimuli. Possibly the most interesting of these phenomena are generalization and transfer effects. When the usual sensory CSs are employed, generalization along sensory continua occurs (this is called sensory generalization), but when the CSs are words, semantic as well as sensory generalization is possible. *Semantic generalization* (sometimes called elective generalization) occurs when CRs are made to words of the same general class as an original CS, from piano to violin, for example, or from cow to other rural words or farm words. Semantic and sensory generalization can be opposed by testing reactions to homophones and synonyms of the original CS. In general, there is more transfer to homophones – from right to write, say, – in younger children, while older subjects transfer more to synonyms – from right to correct.

Sensory and semantic generalization are observed within each class of stimuli, sensory and verbal, respectively. These classes of stimuli, Pavlov referred to as *signalling systems*, the first signalling system being sensory signals and the second signalling system being verbal signals. A third type of generalization, known as *dynamic transmission*, is transfer *between* the signalling systems. In this case, a CR may be established to a sensory stimulus, a red light say, and the ability of the word 'red' to elicit the CR examined. Several Russian studies have demonstrated that dynamic transmission occurs, although in many cases voluntary, emitted, responses rather than elicited CRs have been used.[28]

The importance of dynamic transmission in everyday life can hardly be overestimated. Conditioned responses formed to sensory stimuli in young infants may later be elicited by words as the infants develop, and it is possible that some abnormal clinical symptoms attributed to 'the unconscious' develop in this way. Also not to be overlooked is the value of words in self-control, as when an individual thinks or talks to himself or herself, thereby transferring control from external to internal stimulation. Obviously, generalization from sensations to words depends on prior learning

– the sound 'red' and the colour red must first be associated before a CR to one can generalize to the other.

A form of conditioning that may underlie the various generalization phenomena, dynamic transmission in particular, is *sensory pre-conditioning*. In this instance two stimuli are paired without any particular consequence occurring to their association. In a second stage, one of the stimuli is used as the CS in a conventional conditioning arrangement, and finally the other stimulus is tested to see if it too will elicit the CR. Although many attempts to demonstrate sensory pre-conditioning have failed, some successes have been reported.[29]

Compound conditioned stimuli

Pavlov studied not only single conditioned stimuli but also multiple or compound CSs. All sorts of possible temporal combinations are possible when more than one CS is employed, the limits being simultaneous compounding, when two or more CSs occur together, and successive compounding, when one CS follows another.

Pavlov's studies of higher-order conditioning and conditioned inhibition are early examples of the use of multiple stimuli. They are prototypes of successive and simultaneous compounding respectively, although in the latter case, simultaneity means only overlap, not contiguous onset and offset. In both these cases, a CR is established by reinforcement of one stimulus (the positive CS) and the effects of combining this with an unreinforced (negative) stimulus examined. Pavlov established that conditioned inhibition is developed with comparative ease when the positive stimulus overlaps with the additional stimulus, but that the second stimulus itself acquires secondary positive conditioning properties when there is a pause of about 10 seconds between the offset of the first and the onset of the second stimulus.

I noted Pavlov's concern with analysing the interacting effects of excitation and inhibition with tactile CSs in the illustration of irradiation of inhibition across the brain (Table 4.1). He used multiple tactile stimuli to demonstrate another postulated relationship between excitation and inhibition – *induction*. His evidence for this phenomenon is shown in Table 4.2.

Table 4.2. Data presented as evidence of induction.

Time	Conditioned stimulus applied during 30 seconds	Salivary secretion in drops during 30 seconds	Latent period of the salivary reaction in seconds
4.20 p.m.	Front paw	8	3
4.36 p.m.	Front paw	7.5	3
4.45½ p.m.	Hind paw	0	–
4.45 p.m.	Front paw	12	2
4.58 p.m.	Front paw	5	8
5.10 p.m.	Front paw	6.5	5

From I.P. Pavlov, *Conditioned Reflexes*, 189.

The data in Table 4.2 were collected in the following way: salivation was conditioned to the tactual stimulation of a front paw, and generalization to a similar stimulation of a hind paw inhibited. The table shows that two successive applications of the positive stimulus 16 minutes apart (4.20 p.m. and 4.36 p.m.) produced about 8 drops of conditioned saliva each. Nine minutes later, the inhibitory stimulus, applied to the hind paw, elicited no salivation. Now, from previous findings it would be expected that a wave of irradiated inhibition would leave the cortex in an unreceptive state for further stimulation. However, when the positive stimulus was applied immediately on the termination of the negative stimulus (at 4.45½), an *increase* in the amount of saliva secreted came about. Further stimulation after short intervals of time showed partial inhibition of the positive stimulus, as would be expected from the irradiation of inhibition idea.

How is the increase in excitation at 4.45½ to be explained? Pavlov reasoned that the inhibition of one place in the cortex immediately induces a temporary state of excitation in all others before they are overcome by irradiated inhibition, and that the elevated amount of salivation on the trial at 4.45½ illustrates that temporary excitation. According to Pavlov's analysis, then, any stimulation of the cortex has multiple effects. If the stimulus is excitatory, then (1) its cortical centre becomes excited, (2) by induction all other cortical centres become inhibited, (3) a wave of excitation spreads outwards across the cortex from the original centre. From the other evidence he also argues that (4) this wave concentrates back again to its point of origin. A similar sequence of events, with polarity reversed, is assumed to follow negative (inhibitory) stimulation. This state of affairs is a far cry from Pavlov's original simple conception of 'centres' in the brain.

Pavlov's references to inhibitory and excitatory phenomena and their interactions are theoretical, not empirical, statements. They reflect his assumption of specificity on the part of every stimulus, such that if a stimulus acting alone evokes a CR, but in combination it does not, it follows for him that the second stimulus inhibits the action of the first. However the assumption of specificity may be false, for there is evidence that *compound* conditioning can occur without *component* conditioning.[30] Thus Palladin first conditioned a response to a tactile CS, and then combined this with a thermal CS. The compound elicited a reinforced CR for over 150 trials, but when tested alone, the thermal CS failed to elicit a CR. Pairing the thermal stimulus in a compound CS with the tactile CS did not serve to make the thermal stimulus alone a CS. This phenomenon is known as overshadowing.[31] It is also an example of a whole that is greater than the sum of its parts.

The organism: conditioning and temperament

Pavlov began his investigations of conditioning using dogs, but since then all sorts of organisms have been conditioned including planaria, chicken embryos, and even the human foetus. Certainly, human newborns are conditionable before they are two days old, and there is evidence of increasing conditionability with age in the young. There is less evidence of good conditioning in older adults. All in all very little phylogenetic or ontogenetic comparisons have been made of parameters of the conditioned response.[32] Temperament and personality, on the other hand, have aroused more interest.

Pavlov expressed considerable interest in the differential rate of conditioning in different dogs. He was to refer again and again to the phenomenon, almost always in the context of the build-up of conditioned inhibition in dogs of different temperaments. Dogs of different temperaments condition at different rates. They also extinguish at different rates:

The rate of experimental extinction, measured by the period of time during which a given stimulus must be applied at definite regular intervals without reinforcement before the reflex response becomes zero, depends on numerous conditions. Under the same set of external conditions some animals will have the conditioned reflexes rapidly extinguished, while in others the whole process will be much delayed. In excitable dogs the reflexes are mostly slow of extinction, but in quiet animals extinction is rapid.[33]

Extinction, Pavlov believed, is the result of *internal inhibition* – where excitation in a cortical centre (that of a CS) is blocked by inhibition built up in the same cortical centre. Pavlov also noted temperamental differences in dogs exposed to *external inhibition*, where excitation of one cortical centre (that of the CS) is supposedly inhibited by novel excitation in a different locus in the brain (interference). If it is weak, the novel stimulus evokes an 'investigatory reflex':[34] if strong, the evoked response depends on the type of dog. Pavlov wrote:

> With respect to strong or unusual stimuli, dogs can be divided into two groups. Some respond in a manner which may be termed positive, i.e. aggressively barking furiously and baring their teeth. Others exhibit a defence reaction of a passive nature – they try to get free and run away or they stand like lumps of stone absolutely motionless; and sometimes they will shiver violently and crouch down in the stand; or they may urinate, a most unusual occurrence for dogs while in the stand. In these dogs inhibition predominates.[35]

True to his physiological interests, Pavlov went on to speculate on temperamental types of dogs in terms of properties of the nervous system that he called *strength*, *equilibrium*, and *mobility*. He believed that individual susceptibilities to neurotic breakdowns under conditioning procedures were determined by constitutional differences in the strengths of excitatory and inhibitory tendencies, their mobility and their balance in individual cases. Table 4.3 summarizes his typological system and relates it to Galen's humoral theory of temperaments.[36]

Dogs with weak nervous systems (melancholics, assessed by complex independent conditioning tests) are said to succumb most easily to experimental neurosis, followed by the strong unbalanced (excitatory, choleric) type, with lively, sanguine dogs most resistant

**Table 4.3. Pavlov's typology of nervous systems of dogs based on
strength, balance and mobility of excitatory and inhibitory
higher nervous processes.**

Strength	*Balance*	*Mobility*
Weak (Melancholic)		
or		
Strong ———————	Unbalanced (Choleric)	
	or	
	Balanced —————	Labile (Sanguine)
		or
		Inert (Phlegmatic)

of all to experimental neurosis. When a dog did become neurotic,
Pavlov used sedation by bromides to treat the neurosis, and found
that strong excitatory dogs required much larger bromide doses to
sedate them than did dogs of the weak inhibitory type.

5

Operant Conditioning: Skinner

An alternative to the Pavlovian approach to the stimulus control of behaviour is a line of psychological research initiated by B.F. Skinner in the early 1930s.[1] With this research, originally conducted with laboratory rats, Skinner discovered order in the 'voluntary' behaviour of individual organisms. Although Skinner's reasoning has a scientific history of its own, largely in the field of reflex physiology, its immediate psychological ancestor is the behaviourism of John B. Watson. Watson rejected mentalism as the proper subject-matter of scientific psychology and instead substituted its aim as the prediction and control of behaviour. He reduced S-O-R psychology to S-R psychology. It is important to notice, though, that Watson's concern was with psychology as a *functional* science, a science of cause and effect, not with an existential psychology. He denied the relevance of conscious mentality in the functional control of behaviour, and Skinner has argued the same point of view. So has Freud. Freud attributed control of behaviour not to free will but to an unconscious mentality within the behaver. Skinner attributes behaviour not to free will but to interactions between the organism and its environment. Conscious experience is undeniable and neither Freud nor Skinner has denied it, only looked elsewhere for the causes of behaviour.

Pavlov, Watson and Skinner chose to ignore the traditional inner mental mechanisms of psychology and tried to understand behaviour by looking for ways of bringing it under the control of stimuli in the physical and social environment. Watson promulgated behaviourism in ignorance of Pavlov's early work, but he eventually utilized it in attempting to put his behaviouristic programme into effect. He was among the first to demonstrate the applicability of

Pavlov's conditioning procedures to human behaviour. However, as Skinner pointed out, the scope of Pavlovian conditioning is limited to reflexes, while most human behaviour is 'voluntary'. There are stimuli that will elicit simple reflexes but none that will elicit the behaviour of writing a letter, reading a book or rowing a boat. These behaviours are emitted. Skinner called these activities *operants* (because they operate on the environment) in contrast to Pavlovian *respondent* behaviour (which responds to the environment), and undertook to study the ways in which emitted operants could be brought under stimulus control, just as Pavlov has studied how once neutral stimuli could acquire control over elicited, reflexive behaviour.

Pavlov called a stimulus that came to control elicited behaviour a conditioned stimulus (CS); Skinner called one that controls emitted behaviour a *discriminative stimulus* (S^D). Both kinds of stimuli acquire their properties through differential reinforcement but, as I showed in Chapter 4, reinforcement is not response-dependent in the Pavlovian case. In the operant case, reinforcement depends upon the to-be-conditioned operant. It can be construed as a reward for a response that has been made rather than as a stimulus that elicits a response that is to be made. The principal law of operant conditioning is the Law of Effect.

The Law of Effect was first stated formally by E.L. Thorndike in 1898. It expressed his belief that behaviour followed by a 'reinforcing state of affairs' is learned, or 'stamped-in'. Thorndike's discovery initiated a long line of research on the nature of learning and the necessity of reward for learning to occur. Skinner's work, on the other hand, pertains more to the *maintenance* of behaviour once it occurs, and is more relevant to the psychology of motivation than to the psychology of learning. Even Skinner's later conceptualization of the moulding or *shaping* of behaviour, which bears most closely on traditional conceptions of the learning process, is better regarded as concerned with how behaviour is selected by an environment rather than created by an organism. In this sense, Skinner does for psychology what Darwin did for biology.

Apart from an early foray into a theoretical account of learning, Skinner has vigorously rejected theories about learning and devoted himself to the study of the ways in which stimuli come to control behaviour. Skinner has committed himself to an S-R psychology, but not to the mechanical S-R psychology of Pavlov. Watson argued that the only logical and consistent *functional* psychology is behaviourism, meaning that the only datum of psychology is behaviour and the only independent variables are stimuli, and Skinner has defended the same point of view. This variety of S-R psychology claims only that mentality is irrelevant to a complete analysis of the factors that control behaviour; it does *not* assert a mechanical connection between S and R, or an 'empty-minded' organism.[2]

Skinner realized that stimuli could *set the occasion* for behaviour without necessarily eliciting it, and insisted that behaviour could be brought under stimulus control without knowledge of the connecting route from S to R. That is, he founded a functional psychology independently of physiology, exactly as Freud had done. And also like Freud, he extended his analysis to social and individual human psychology.

Establishing an operant

An operant cannot be reinforced until it is emitted, so its first appearance must be spontaneous. The spontaneous emission rate of a response is known as its *operant rate*, and control over it is not demonstrated until the conditioned rate of emission differs from the operant rate.

What constitutes 'different from' in Skinner's research is not determined by statistical analysis of the combined data of groups of animals, but by the consistent reproducibility of the performance of single animals under controlled conditions. To this end, sources of errors are minimized by careful attention to apparatus design and experimental procedures rather than by statistical separation of 'true' data from random error. By comparison with traditional psychological research procedures, this is analogous to a chemist using a pure sample instead of several containing impurities in trying to discover the properties of a particular chemical. The success of Skinner's tactic is demonstrated by the stability of experimental data generated by his methods.[3]

To begin with, Skinner, like Pavlov, used the 'animal model' approach to the study of behaviour. In particular, he watched hungry rats working for food, using first a runway and later a chamber (Skinner Box) equipped with a horizontal bar and a noisy food delivery mechanism. A hungry rat is placed in the chamber and the magazine is set to dispense a pellet of food when it presses the bar. The response is *immediately* reinforced. For Skinner, immediacy of reinforcement is the trick that serves to condition the response. He demonstrates conditioning visually after the manner of Figure 1. The figure is a cumulative record of responses on the ordinate with the passage of time shown along the abscissa.[4] The curve shows immediately orderliness in behaviour and the rate of responding, which is Skinner's measure of response strength.

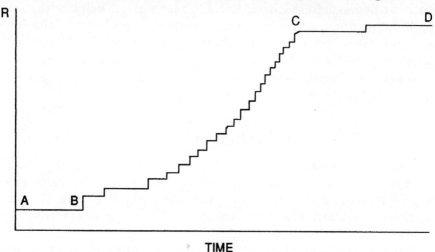

TIME

Figure 5.1. A cumulative record. The first portion of the record (from A to B) indicates the passage of time with no responses. From B to C the record rises with each reinforced response. At C, reinforcement is discontinued and the record levels off from C to D.

Just as Pavlov did not discover respondent conditioning so Skinner was not the first to teach an animal with food reinforcement. Guy de Maupassant described the method in a short story in which a dog was trained to avenge the murder of its master:

> The widow of Paolo Saverini lived ... alone with her son Antoine and their dog Semillante ...
> One evening after a dispute, Antoine Saverini was killed ... by Nicolas Ravolati who the same night fled to Sardinia.

When the old woman received the body of her child ... she promised revenge ...

She had in her yard an old barrel ... She emptied it and turned it over, making it fast to the soil by means of some stakes and stones; then she chained Semillante in this niche ...

The dog howled all day and all night. The old woman carried her some water in the morning ... But nothing more; no soup no bread ... She took some old clothes ... and filled them ... to simulate a human body ... Having stuck a stick in the ground before Semillante's niche, she bound the manikin to it ... Then the old woman went to the butcher's and bought a long piece of black pudding. She returned home ... and cooked this pudding. Semillante, excited, bounded about and frothed at the mouth, her eyes fixed upon the meat ...

Next the woman made a cravat for the straw man of this smoking sausage. She wound it many times around his neck ... When this was done she unchained the dog.

With a formidable leap the beast reached the manikin's throat and ... began to tear him to pieces ...

For three months she accustomed the dog to this kind of struggle ... She did not chain her now but set her upon the manikin with a gesture.

She taught her to tear him, to devour him, even without anything eatable hung around his throat. She would give her afterward, as a recompense, the pudding she had cooked for her.

Whenever she perceived the manikin Semillante growled and turned her eyes toward her mistress who would cry: 'Go!' ... at the same time raising her finger.

When she thought the right time had come, Mother Severini ... presented herself at a baker's and asked where Nicolas Ravolati lived ... He was working alone at the back of his shop.

The old woman opened the door and called:

'Hey, Nicolas!'

He turned around; then, loosing the dog, she cried out:

'Go! Go! Devour him! Devour him!'

The animal, excited, threw herself upon him and seized him by the throat ... until it was in shreds ...[5]

This fictional example illustrates Skinner's scientific system, operant chaining and stimulus control.

Stimulus control

The control of behaviour through reinforcement is possible only *after* the behaviour occurs. While the behaviour is reinforced, it continues with some strength, but without reinforcement, it weakens to its operant level. In that case, the behaviour is no longer available for further strengthening until it occurs again spontaneously. This is control of a very low order. A higher order of control is when a stimulus that *precedes* it determines when the behaviour occurs. This happens when a response is reinforced only in the presence of one stimulus and extinguished in its absence. In that case, the behaviour occurs when the stimulus occurs, otherwise not, giving the appearance that the stimulus elicits the response. But the stimulus only sets the occasion for reinforcement of the response. It is not an eliciting stimulus (CS) but a discriminative stimulus (S^D). Skinner gives the example of a man reaching for a pencil. He reaches when the pencil is visible (S^D) but not when it cannot be seen. The response is not made unless the pencil is present, but the pencil does not evoke the response.

Reaching for the pencil is voluntary in the ordinary sense. The rat's bar-pressing behaviour is voluntary in the same sense. Skinner argues that everyday human voluntary behaviour is controlled in the same way as the experimental animal's is in the 'Skinner Box', not by a hypothetical will but by actual consequences. By Skinner's account, most human everyday behaviours – stopping at a red light, walking through a door, sitting on a chair, reading a book, drinking a beer – are *discriminated operants*.

Operant chaining

Normal behaviour is complex. Even simple bar pressing is part of a response chain, because after each response the animal must at least consume the reinforcer. A more detailed analysis of a reinforced bar press indicates that there are several activities involved: approaching the bar, pressing the bar, moving to the reinforcement magazine, and consuming the reinforcer. When an animal is trained in an experimental chamber in which response manipulandum and reinforcement magazine are not immediately adjacent, special attention must be paid to the way in which the complete sequence of activities is established. At first, the animal is placed in the chamber and fed freely from the magazine; it learns where to eat. Then it is taught *when* it can eat, and then it is trained by differential reinforcement to press the bar. The total procedure involves *chaining* and *shaping* or *approximation training*.

Chaining refers to the forging of the behaviour link by link backwards from the goal: sight of food in magazine leads to eating; sound of magazine leads to a magazine approach; bar press produces sound of magazine. Shaping refers to the selective reinforcement of closer and closer approximation to the desired response. The first bar press is therefore not left entirely to chance, but is gradually shaped from a crude to a skilled performance. A child's first words are shaped like this, and its further education follows the same procedure. First the child is motivated, then it is trained backwards from its goal by chaining and approximations to make the desired response. This is programmed learning. Skinner employed it in the development of teaching machines, but he gave an exemplary account of backward chaining with a rat in his first book, *The Behavior of Organisms*.

> As a sort of *tour de force* I have trained a rat to execute an elaborate series of responses suggested by recent work on anthropoid apes. The behaviour consists of pulling a string to obtain a marble from a rack, picking the marble up with the fore-paws, carrying it to a tube projecting two inches above the floor of the cage, lifting it to the top of the tube, and dropping it inside.[6]

At first, the rat was fed when it touched the marble, then it had to push the marble through a tube flush with the table, then the tube was raised, and finally the animal had to pull the string to obtain the marble. By this example, Skinner displays his interest in shaping complex behaviour rather than in assessing an organism's mental capacities, as Kohler had done with apes.[7]

Discrimination and differentiation

When Pavlov described responses conditioned to one stimulus but not to another, he used discrimination and differentiation interchangeably, but in Skinner's system they refer to different operations: the discrimination of a stimulus and the differentiation of a response.

Skinner calls a stimulus discriminated when an organism behaves differently in its presence and in its absence. Differentiation of a response is when reinforcers follow one response but not others. Differentiation may be quite crude, as when an animal must press a lever rather than pull a chain for food, or it can be quite refined, as in 'shaping' or approximation training. Differentiation describes the shaping of complex skills; discrimination describes the occasions for their use.

The interplay of discrimination and differentiation can be observed in games like tennis. Players aim their rackets at the ball rather than at their opponents, and at where the ball is rather than where it was (discrimination); and they learn to control strokes so that the ball lands in the opponent's court instead of the window of the house next door (differentiation).

Categories of reinforcers

The fate of operant behaviour depends on its consequences – states of affairs that may actually be produced by the behaviour or which may merely be coincidental with it. Skinner defines a reinforcer as a stimulus that strengthens the behaviour that precedes it; he does not believe that punishment weakens behaviour, but that it only suppresses it temporarily. In the examples I have given so far, it has been the *production* of stimuli that has maintained responding. This is positive reinforcement. But the *removal* of stimulation may also be reinforcing – as in the case of threatening or painful stimuli.[8] This is *negative* reinforcement in Skinner's language. This language does not leave Skinner at liberty to say that behaviour is strengthened *because* it is reinforced. This circularity is avoidable only if a reinforcer is defined independently of the behaviour it strengthens.[9]

Reinforcers may be positive or negative; they may also be primary or secondary. It is not always easy to maintain a clear distinction between primary and secondary reinforcers, but, in general, primary reinforcers serve some unlearned biological functions whereas secondary, or conditioned, reinforcing properties are acquired. Food and water, therefore, are primary reinforcers for hungry and thirsty organisms, while lights and sounds become reinforcers only through association with these or other primary reinforcers.[10] Association with primary reinforcers requires precisely the arrangement necessary to establish stimuli as conditioned or discriminative stimuli, and we have already seen how Pavlov transferred control over a respondent to a higher-order CS by using a first-order CS as a secondary reinforcer.

Secondary reinforcers are not ends in themselves, but signals that primary reinforcement may be forthcoming. When primary reinforcement is intermittent, only secondary reinforcing consequences of many emitted responses may be observed, and unless a sufficiently large segment of behaviour is recorded, inferences about ultimate sources of reinforcement are likely to be mistaken.[11]

Freud also concluded that the origins of behaviour are not always obvious, although he may have been unnecessarily restrictive in regarding the ultimate ends of behaviour as sexual or destructive. Skinner also has been restrictive in confining his reinforcer to food for hungry captive animals. Although Skinner has generalized his laboratory findings to a utopian society and to human freedom and dignity, at bottom these findings come out of a prison economy. Freud, of course, generalized his findings from the sick bed, or couch.

Maintaining an operant

Reinforcement is not necessary every time an act occurs. Not every visit to a favourite restaurant is a delight, and not every day at work is immediately paid. Yet we continue eating and working. Non-reinforcement of an act weakens it, but as extinction is not usually immediate, withholding a single reinforcer seldom leads to total cessation of a response. Provided this point is not reached, reinforcement can be reinstated and the response reconditioned. Skinner originally called this periodic reinforcement, and studied the maintenance of behaviour when it is reinforced intermittently according to the ratio of responses per reinforcer, or to the intervals of non-reinforcement between reinforcers. These are ratio and interval schedules, which are the bases of the variety of complex schedules of reinforcement described below. In them, the ratio components define what behaviour is reinforced (response topography), and the interval components specify times when reinforcement is available.

Schedules of reinforcement[12]

In radical behaviourism, schedules of reinforcement occupy the same logical position as mental architecture occupies in psychoanalysis: in psychoanalysis the structure of the mind is the determinant of behaviour, in Skinner's system, behaviour is determined by the structure of the environment. In both cases the nature of the structure is dynamic – the struggle between intrapsychic forces in the one case and the consequence of responses in the other. Skinner has described a large number of response-consequence schedules, some as examples of everyday situations, and some as techniques for unravelling the stimulus control of behaviour.

Fixed and variable ratios

Ratio schedules specify the amount of behaviour required for reinforcement. They may be fixed (FR), where the reinforced response topography is always the same, or variable (VR), where a range of topographies is reinforced. Over an extended period of time, the number of responses required per reinforcer may be the same on both these types of schedule, but they maintain different patterns of behaviour owing to local variations in reinforcement density in the variable-ratio case. In that case, performance is not so stereotyped as in the fixed-ratio example.

Very large response topographies are possible with very few reinforcers. Thus, Findley and Brady[13] trained a chimpanzee to emit 120,000 responses per reinforcer. After every 4,000 responses, the stimuli associated with reinforcement were presented but reinforcement was withheld. On only the 30th occasion on which these stimuli appeared was a primary reinforcer (banana pellet) delivered. The pellet probably did not replenish the energy expended to obtain it.

Naturally a good deal of prior training was required before this level of output was reached. Using smaller ratios of 4,000, Findley and Brady also demonstrated that a chimpanzee would respond more quickly and consistently when the reinforcement signal ap-

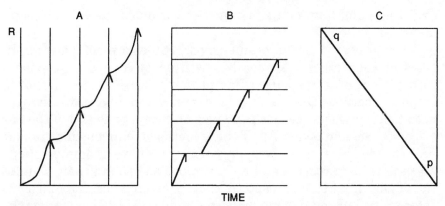

Figure 5.2.

(A) *Fixed intervals.* Reinforcers are scheduled for whenever a rising cumulative record crosses the vertical lines. Response rate is typically low after reinforcement and high just before the next reinforcer is due. The curve is known as a scallop.

(B) *Fixed ratios.* Reinforcers are scheduled for whenever a cumulative record crosses the horizontal lines. Response rate is typically high up to reinforcement, after which there is a brief 'post-reinforcement' pause.

(C) *Interlocking schedule.* Reinforcement is scheduled for whenever a rising cumulative record crosses the solid line. Rotation of this line to p changes the schedule to FI; rotation to q changes it to FR.

peared after every 400 responses (but unaccompanied by reinforcement) than when the signal was omitted, except at the end of the total ratio. When the with-and-without-signal conditions were signalled by red and green lights, respectively, the animal learned to press a button to select the red light condition. A person observing this final performance could not guess how it arose. In the human case, a probable guess would appeal to an intrapsychic personality or to a preference for red over green.

Fixed and variable intervals

Interval schedules bear the same relationship to temporal parameters as ratio schedules bear to response parameters. Response rates generated by interval schedules, however, are much lower than those generated by ratio schedules because, in the interval case, rate of reinforcement is not dependent on rate of response, as it is in the case of ratio schedules. Piecework is reinforcement on a ratio schedule; weekly wages are reinforcement on a fixed-interval; Skinner cites gambling as an instance of variable-interval reinforcement.

Operant responses maintained by schedules are not exact duplicates of each other. Skinner has written of *classes of responses* rather than of 'a response'. Bar pressing, for instance, is not 'a response' because the bar may be depressed in a variety of ways – with more or less force, with one paw or both, at one end of the bar or the other, and so on. All of these methods of displacing the bar are regarded as a class of response if they all have a common effect, and the term 'a response' is a convenient shorthand that includes the whole class. How a response class is established is a matter of conjecture that could bring modern cognitive psychology under the behavioural umbrella.

A response, then, is defined not structurally by its form, but functionally by its effects.

Theory of reinforcement schedules

There is more to reinforcement schedules than the relatively sterile technicalities of the examples I have described. In operant psychology, they carry the weight of the metaphorical memory storage of cognitive psychologies; they function as the radical unconscious of radical behaviourism equivalent to the dynamic unconscious of psychoanalysis.

Freud invented the dynamic unconscious to provide temporal continuity between early childhood experiences and non-rational, contemporary behaviour. Reinforcement schedules serve the same purpose. Schedules and the unconscious alike must explain how past experience determines ongoing behaviour. Schedules do this by describing directly organism-environment transactions, but the Freudian unconscious invites additional inquiry into its structure. Forgetting its status as metaphor, Freud and Jung soon differed over the nature of the unconscious, and psychoanalysts have proposed revised guesses about its structure ever since. There are no such structural problems with reinforcement schedules, for they are specifiable objective transactions without metaphorical implications. The problem with schedules is to explain how they function. The explanation is concerned with how forms of behaviour originate, how they are selected and maintained, and how non-reinforced responses are distributed in time.

The theory of reinforcement schedules originated in the psychology of learning, but it is not a theory of learning. Learning is to do with error and success, with the practice that is supposed to make perfect; reinforcement schedules are about the maintenance of behaviour once it has occurred, its modification, and its rate and probability of occurrence. Schedules are concerned with the distribution of behaviour in time. Schedules of reinforcement affect the establishment of behaviours and mould their forms, but the behaviours are not learned acquisitions in the ordinary sense. Reinforced behaviours are behaviours shaped out of prior performance, not behaviours added from scratch to a *tabula rasa*.

In one sense, the theory of reinforcement schedules is the theory of how temporal patterns of behaviour maintained by these schedules come about. A theory of schedules of reinforcement in this sense was proposed by Ferster and Skinner in their book, *Schedules of Reinforcement*, published in 1957. It explained the occurrences of non-reinforced responses solely on the basis of events at the time of reinforcement. In the Ferster-Skinner theory, these events are the four basic processes of conditioning: reinforcement and extinction; stimulus discrimination; response differentiation; and conditioned reinforcement. However, according to Herbert Jenkins, events at the time of reinforcement alone may not be sufficient to account for the appearance of responses on other occasions. He suggested that additional concepts 'concerned with grouping or organization in sequences are needed'. This suggestion implies another meaning of reinforcement schedule theory.[14]

In the second meaning, schedules are not just intermittent occasions of individual events, but environmental fields that interact with and modulate behaviour.[15] The theory at this level is that it is *schedules per se*, not individual events that govern behaviour. Such a theory of reinforcement schedules is a proposition that the sources of behaviour lie in unconscious transactions between persons and environments in a stream-of-behaviour field, not in psychodynamic metaphorical structures possessed by the individual.[16] It is a holistic theory consistent with existential being-in-the-world.

Verbal behaviour

The formal ingredients of a functional analysis of operant behaviour are discriminative stimulus, response and reinforcement. Early experimental demonstrations of this paradigm were restricted to examinations of the control of relatively simple peripheral operants by single publicly observable discriminative stimuli established by way of differential reinforcement delivered mechanically. Later elaborations incorporated more complex responses, as exemplified by chains, and the effects of scheduling reinforcement in various ways, but the functional analysis of behaviour has been carried to its highest pitch in Skinner's account of verbal behaviour in operant terms.[17]

Although Skinner's account ostensibly pertains to a different quality of response from tradition – verbal instead of motor behaviour – it also extends the notions of discriminative stimuli and reinforcement in important ways. In the case of discriminative stimuli, consideration is given to private as well as to public stimuli, and also to the problem of multiple stimulus control, whereby the same form of a response may be determined separately and independently by different stimuli. In the case of reinforcing stimuli, the notion of mechanical reinforcement is supplemented by that of social reinforcement – a condition in which reinforcement is contingent upon the behaviour of a 'reinforcing community' instead of arising directly as the consequence of an instrumental act. Of course, when a second individual is required to reinforce the behaviour of a first, reinforcement is likely to be less reliable than when it is produced mechanically. Reinforcement schedules are ubiquitous in social situations. In language learning, they underpin Sullivan's consensual validation.

Acquisition

Verbal behaviour is usually regarded as a higher form of human activity than the performance of motor skills. When an infant learns to walk, or a child to skate, we are content to describe the behaviour as walking or skating and leave it at that. When it learns to talk, we envisage more than a mere involvement of the vocal apparatus comparable to the role of limbs in walking and skating.

We imagine that it learns that words have meanings and that it can use these meanings to convey its ideas, however rudimentary.

Social reinforcement

Skinner maintains that meanings are not properties carried by words, or words expressions of ideas. If an idea is the cause of an utterance then the idea remains to be explained, so unless there is evidence of the idea apart from the utterance, no explanation is forthcoming. The emission of the utterance must be attributed to another source, and this source, says Skinner, is a listener, whose behaviour is what determines what the utterance shall mean. As Skinner puts it, when we say that we know what a word means, we are not describing the word (dependent variable) but the conditions under which it is emitted (independent variables). The listener sets the occasion (S^D) for the utterance, and reinforces it if it is appropriate to the situation in which it occurs.

A child comes to emit the word *ball* in the presence of a round rubber object, and *bell* in the presence of a shiny object that tinkles, because it is reinforced by approval or by being given the object when the appropriate response is made. If the child says '*ball*', it is given the ball, and this serves to strengthen the response for future use. When the next appropriate occasion occurs the response will be emitted in exactly the same way as if the child had learned to reach for the ball (mechanical reinforcement). The meaning of the word is exactly determined by the behaviour of the listener. There appears to be a difference between saying and reaching if *bell* is said when the child should say *ball*. We are inclined to say that he *means ball* in a way that we would not say that he means a different reach, but no more is involved than the degree of differentiation of the response.

Verbal behaviour is not necessarily behaviour that expresses mental activity on the part of a speaker, and it does not demand explanation in terms that differ in principle from those applicable to non-verbal behaviour. Verbal and non-verbal behaviour differ in the conditions required for their reinforcement: social and mechanical, respectively. So verbal behaviour is not confined to vocalization but can take any form that eventually requires an audience for its effect. Reading, writing and arithmetic are all verbal behaviours, as are gestures, grimaces, insignias of rank, and the motor-behaviour of waving semaphore flags or tapping a telegraph key. The proper distinction is not between verbal and motor behaviour but between verbal and non-verbal behaviour. The distinction is not in the *form* (topography) of the response but in the kind of reinforcement it receives.

Generalized social reinforcement

Social reinforcement is not only less reliable than mechanical reinforcement, it is also less specifically related to particular states of deprivation. Thus agreement, praise, attention, or merely the presence of an audience, may reinforce certain kinds of verbal behaviour, and do so in the absence of specifiable deprivation in a way that primary reinforcers like food or water do not. Social reinforcers are usually conditioned reinforcers but they are not *just* conditioned reinforcers, they are *generalized conditioned reinforcers*.

Generalized conditioned reinforcers are established in the same way as simple conditioned reinforcers, but they do not rely on a single state of deprivation. If a red light, for example, becomes a discriminative stimulus (S^D) for eating, it will be a simple conditioned reinforcer for any behaviour that makes eating possible, but its effects will be restricted to occasions when the organism is hungry. If the same red light is also made an S^D for drinking, it will now be a secondary reinforcer whether the organism is hungry or thirsty. Its effect is freed from reliance on either form of deprivation, and its reinforcing property is said to be generalized. Although this example is very primitive, it is plain that conditioned reinforcers may be generalized as far as we please. Few parents consider themselves as reinforcers for their children's behaviour, but parental cooperation is necessary for the satisfaction of most of an infant's needs. Sullivan (Chapter 3), makes much of this. By the very process of keeping an infant alive, adults establish themselves as powerful generalized reinforcers.

It is also possible for a child to reinforce itself. In this case, Skinner calls the reinforcement *intrinsic*. A self-spoken *Good boy!*, he says, will reinforce just as much as praise from a parent after an appropriate conditioning history. There are obvious advantages in this, for it frees behaviour from the constraints of audience control, but there are disadvantages too, for intrinsic reinforcement may follow the wish as much as the deed. And also the fear, as with irrational phobias.

Multiple stimulus control

Traditional accounts of behaviour, verbal and non-verbal, take more account of its form than of its functional properties. But the poverty of formal emphasis is exposed by hysterical reactions, in which a word may be remembered under some conditions but not others, and aphasias in which a word may be known when written but not when spoken. These situations require functional, not formal, analysis.

From a formal, topographical, point of view it is strange that a person can utter a word such as *book* on some occasions but not on others. If the word is taken to express the idea, then the failure is incomprehensible. From a functional standpoint the mystery is lessened. Consider three kinds of verbal behaviour that Skinner has named *echoic, textual*, and *intraverbal*. Echoic is pronouncement of the word heard, textual is pronouncement of a word read, and intraverbal is pronouncement of a word in a phrase. Each of these pronouncements may take the same form, *stripes* for example, but the occasioning stimuli may be: *Repeat after me – STRIPES!* (echoic), *Read this word – STRIPES* (textual) or *Complete the phrase: STARS AND* —— (intraverbal). The response must be established separately to each of these three situations. The word STRIPES is multiply controlled and an injury may damage one source of control while leaving the others intact, as in aphasia.

Mands and tacts

More complex controlling contingencies exist in the cases of *mands* and *tacts*, for these differ not only in prior stimulus control but also in their reinforcing consequences. A mand is a word that specifies its own reinforcer. It need have no observable occasioning stimulus; its reinforcing consequence is behaviour of the listener. Skinner coined mand by contracting command, demand, countermand; in all cases the mand specifies what the listener should do – 'Please get me a drink.' The listener reinforces by complying.

A tact, on the other hand is a word that describes its own discriminative stimulus. That is, the form of a tact is occasioned by a prior stimulus in the presence of which it is appropriate – 'Here is a glass.' The consequences of a tact are not specified as they are by a mand. Most commonly, tacting is naming, and the term is contracted from contacting, or making contact with.

Mands and tacts exemplify different functional properties of utterances regardless of form. Consider the word *water* emitted as a mand and as a tact in the three-stage stimulus-response-reinforcement paradigm. The stimulus occasioning *water* as a mand is the aversive condition of thirst, and the reinforcement is receipt of a glass of water. No water need exist in the environment prior to the response, and the word specifies the behaviour of the listener. When *water* is emitted as a tact the occasioning stimulus is specified by the physical presence of water, but the reinforcing behaviour of the listener is not determined. The total speech episode in each case can be represented as follows:

	Prior stimulus	Response	Reinforcement
Mand	Thirst	'Water'	Listener gives it
Tact	Water present	'Water'	Listener agrees

These episodes depict two different circumstances under which the same response is emitted. They also exemplify two ways in which it is acquired, and a response acquired according to one set of circumstances may not be available in the other. A child able to tact water by saying 'That is water' does not automatically possess the mand form 'I want water', although it is possible for the two forms to develop more or less together.

Novel responses

The technique of shaping, already described for the moulding of animal behaviour, is also available for sharpening the form of verbal responses. However, this is not the only way a verbal repertoire is established. Encouraging echoic behaviour is another. Echoic behaviour itself can be acquired, and this necessitates reinforcing productions that match a teacher's example. At first the match may be imprecise, but by gradually demanding closer and closer matches for reinforcement, a teacher can shape echoic behaviour by making reinforcement contingent upon the *similarity* of pupil's and teacher's productions *per se*, rather than upon the actual response of the pupil. Eventually any novel response emitted by the teacher will then be matched (echoed, imitated) by the pupil, and separate shaping of each item in a verbal repertoire is by-passed. A laboratory parallel is called *matching-to-sample*.

Other forms of response novelty Skinner has called *extended tacts*. The concept of extension corresponds to that of generalization of non-verbal behaviour insofar as behaviour occurs in situations other than that in which it was initially conditioned. Two forms of extended tacts are *generic extensions* and *metaphorical extensions*. Generic extension is what is usually called concept formation. It stems from the fact that many stimuli are present on occasions of reinforcement. Hence a child reinforced for tacting *table* emits the response in the presence of a multiplicity of stimuli that make up the table. If the tact is systematically established in the presence of several different tables, then some stimulus properties will consistently accompany reinforcement while others will not. Those that regularly accompany reinforcement define the category or concept 'table' and will control the response when an unfamiliar table is named without prompting. Generic extension is not involved when a response is made for the first time ever, only when it is made for the first time in a novel situation.

Metaphorical extensions differ from generic extensions only insofar as some of the stimulus properties accompanying reinforcement of the original response are appropriate to other objects and events. Deep water is often still, and 'deep' may be extended metaphorically to describe an individual who is silent and still. Metaphors must be largely novel to qualify as extended tacts. If they are borrowed from literary sources, they resemble textual, echoic or intraverbal behaviour.

Parallel with extended tacts, Skinner has described *extended mands*. These are utterances that are 'irrational' in the sense of having no intrinsic connection with reinforcement. They may be considered novel only in the sense that they are inappropriate to the conditions in which they occur. Thus *Stop Thief!* is a mand emitted without much chance of reinforcement, as is the mand *Go to the devil!* The responses survive as extensions of other mands that have been appropriately reinforced before.

Private stimulus control

Behaviour is brought under stimulus control by means of differential reinforcement. When a response is reinforced in the presence of a stimulus but not in its absence, the response comes to occur with high probability when the stimulus is present, but only rarely otherwise. However, although this principle is sound and is supported by a massive amount of experimental evidence, a practical problem exists when the controlling stimuli are private. A psychology concerned only with observable responses made to public stimuli faces no peculiar problems as a natural science of behaviour, because an observer can tell when the stimulus is present and when the behaviour occurs, and so can reinforce accordingly. But such a psychology would exclude the very phenomenon that brought it into being – consciousness. The early behaviourists were inclined to solve the problem of consciousness by neglecting it, but it is possible to include conscious phenomena in a functional behaviourism by considering them as private stimuli and responses. What must be discovered is how reinforcement can be made contingent upon stimuli not available to the reinforcing community. Skinner gives several examples.

Public correlates

How can one organism differentially reinforce the behaviour of another organism made to stimuli not directly available to the reinforcing organism? How, for example, can the listener appropriately reinforce the mand *water* when he or she cannot experience the speaker's thirst that sets the occasion for the response? How can a child learn to say that it is thirsty, or that its tooth aches, when there are no public thirsts or aches to guide the reinforcing behaviour of the teacher? The answer is that there usually *are* public correlates of private events. One possibility is the collateral behaviour of the speaker. Reinforcement by sympathetic attention and help is unlikely to be forthcoming to the grinning playful child who claims to have a toothache. If, however, its claim is supported by grimaces and a swollen jaw, that is another matter. The occasion for social reinforcement is not set by the private experience of the child but by the public behaviour collateral with it (grimacing), or as a second possibility, by accompanying public stimuli (swollen jaw).

This second possibility is also exemplified when a blind man learns to tact the world. When the blind man learns the names of objects, the stimulus events controlling his utterances are tactual. They are private to the blind man and are not available to a teacher, whose responses are made to visual cues. The blind man feels the object and names it (usually echoically), and the teacher reinforces the correct response by agreement. The public verbal response is made to private tactual sensations, but differential reinforcement is possible because there are public accompanying stimuli (the sight of the object) available to the teacher. The drama of this example is that the experiences of teacher and pupil are in different sense modalities. But they need not be, for when a child learns to call an animal a cat, its view of the cat is private and from a different perspective from that of the adult who supplies the reinforcement.

Impure tacts and magical mands

In the case of a tact such as 'water', or any other public stimulus, the teacher can discriminate when to give and when not to give reinforcement. But suppose the stimulus is private, such as 'anxious'? Now the teacher can only differentially reinforce the utterance on the basis of some public behaviour of the speaker that accompanies it, such as a frown or a tear. If the teacher is misled and reinforces inappropriately then the learner learns an impure tact and inappropriately describes his or her private experience. Insofar as impure tacts are most likely to be acquired in childhood, psychoanalysis and behavioural analysis share a common interest in this period of development. Behaviour analysts do not believe in childhood repression, like Freud, but in childhood failures in learning, like Jung and Sullivan. Impure tacts are parataxic distortion.

Mands may also be acquired inappropriately, this time, perhaps, by a speaker listening to himself or herself. In this case, the mand is extended 'magically' to include unavailable reinforcers, as with wishful thinking and delusions of grandeur. As Skinner puts it, 'Having effectively manded bread and butter, [the speaker] goes on to mand the jam.'

The acquisition of magical mands is more likely in adolescence and adulthood than in early childhood, as more and more social demands are placed on an individual then than in early childhood. If the young child says, 'I am sick' it will likely do so as an ordinary tact; the same statement in an older person would be a magical mand if it were an implied appeal for help.

Private events

Descriptions of conscious experience may also arise through the processes of generic and metaphorical extension of tacts described above. In these ways the language of inner experience is not conditioned by differential reinforcement contingent upon private stimuli but upon public stimuli as in the normal acquisition of a tact. The sensation generated by grasping a hot object is called *burning* in the same way as a table comes to be called a table – reinforcement is supplied by a listener aware of the appropriate public accompaniments of the sensation. When a pain in the chest is later described as a *burning sensation*, the phrase is either a generic or a metaphorical extension of the previously acquired tact, according to the precise quality of the sensation. There are other extensions of tacts that Skinner describes, but whichever one is involved in a given instance, the important point is that descriptions of quite private experiences may be acquired through the extension of tacts generated by differential reinforcement on the basis of public stimulus events.

Another kind of verbalization influenced by private events is when a speaker describes not a feeling but an action. If one says 'I am wiggling my toes', this fact is not evident to a listener in the normal course of events; but the statement would originally have been acquired when the toe wriggling was evident and nothing more is involved than that the behaviour is now disguised, either by means of socks and shoes or because the movement is too slight to be detected by another observer. The same may be said about the comment 'I am thinking about an apple.' The thinking behaviour may be no more than an attenuated version of behaviour that had earlier occurred in sufficient strength to be observable.

Supplementary stimuli

Insufficient control

Skinner has discussed *formal* and *thematic* prompts and *probes* as sources of supplementary strength for a weak verbal operant.

Formal prompts are direct stimuli for behaviour under weak intraverbal control. A lecturer may begin, for example, 'The wavelength of blue light is ... er ... er ...' and glance at his notes before completing the sentence '... 460 millimicrons.' Additional strength for the end of the sentence is gained from the written note, and the response is textual rather than intraverbal as it would have been had the whole sentence been 'remembered'. A similar formal prompt could have been provided by a whisper from the audience, in which case the final phrase would have been echoic.

When questioning his audience, the lecturer is more likely to provide *thematic prompts*, which are hints such that the lecturer increases the likelihood of a correct response without actually supplying it. A dialogue might run:

Q. 'What is the wavelength of blue light?'
A. (No response)

Q. 'All right, what are the limits of the visible spectrum?'
A. 'From about 400 to 700 millimicrons.'

Q. 'The reds are the longer wavelengths, which end is blue?'
A. 'The shortest, Oh, I remember, blue is 460 millimicrons.'

A similar thematic prompt might have been supplied by a suitable drawing.

Probes are less direct ways of teasing out verbal behaviour that is either weekly controlled or suppressed through possible punishing consequences. They encompass what are usually called projective tests or techniques, and are also involved in the acts of

creation and discovery. The best known formal probe is the Rorschach Test. This is a series of ink blots that an examinee is asked
to interpret. In the presence of the blot the examinee emits textual
responses that might not be emitted under other sources of control,
and these responses are supposed to be indicative of the personality
dynamics of the responder.

Examples of *thematic probes* in personality analysis are the
Thematic Apperception Test and the Word Association Test, which
are also common projective techniques. In the former, examinees
are required to invent brief stories on the basis of ambiguous
incidents depicted in pictures; in the latter, single word stimuli are
presented to which the examinee is supposed to respond with the
first word that the stimulus calls to mind. Personality descriptions
are then constructed from complex formal and thematic (content)
analyses of the examinee's productions. Jung, in particular, employed this methodology. Freud's interpretations of free
associations are examples of thematic probes.

A controversial aspect of contemporary educational theory is a
change from reliance on formal probes to imaginative use of thematic prompts in teaching. The change parallels the difference
between rote and insightful learning, and expository and hypothetical modes of teaching. Rote learning and expository teaching shape
echoic and textual behaviour that becomes intraverbal when it is
thoroughly learned. When the pupil demonstrates weak responding
(he cannot remember the answer to a question) he is either further
drilled in the material (formal prompt: echoic) or invited to search
out the answer in a book (formal prompt: textual). Other teaching
methods emphasize the realm of possibilities (the hypothetical
mode of teaching) over the realm of actualities (expository mode),
and the teacher provides thematic probes – *suppose the Spanish
Armada had defeated the English fleet* – rather than the formal
prompt – *Drake defeated the Spanish Armada in 1588*. This method
does not imply that factual knowledge is of no consequence, only
that if you look after the possibilities the facts will take care of
themselves.[18]

Multiple control

Prompts and probes are ways of supplementing the strength of verbal responses that otherwise would not be emitted. There are also verbal productions that occur because of control from several sources. Puns, metaphors and slips of the tongue are examples. In Mark Antony's request to the citizens of Rome, 'Nay, press not so upon me; stand far off ', we may conjecture that *press* is occasioned not only from the physical pressure of the citizens requested to stand far off, but also because they were pressing Antony to read the dead Caesar's will. Similarly the word *corn* in the comment 'My eyes are tired; they feel as though they have corn in them', was probably emitted through supplementary strength from *cornea* added to the actual sensation in that region of the eye.

Slips of the tongue, or parapraxes, are usually regarded as the special province of Freudian psychoanalysis, so much so that they are colloquially described as Freudian slips. Through the pressure of tradition, Freud turned to the unconscious to explain parapraxes. The behaviourists have not responded to this pressure. Consequently what to the psychoanalyst is an exemplification of the unconscious, to the behaviourist is a sign of weak or multiple stimulus control.

Rules

Early verbal behaviour is contingency-shaped; later it may be rule-governed. Contingency-shaping is the sharpening (a metaphorical extension) of behaviour by its effects, from, say, *wawa* to *mama*. It is direct shaping of behaviour by its consequences, as in most of the cases discussed so far. These cases could be extended to include writing one's name, riding a bicycle, walking, swimming, writing a poem or painting a work of art. In all these examples, the child, the athlete, the poet or the artist creates the behaviour from its consequences. But frequently some help is required. To become a good swimmer, writer or painter, considerable training is required. This training involves learning skills and objectives from teachers who themselves learned how others succeeded in the past. Skinner calls such learned behaviour rule-governed.[19]

Infant talking is contingency-shaped; grammatical writing is rule-governed. Unless it is a direct quotation, a sentence, therefore, is a rule-governed production in its structure and contingency-shaped when it is turned into literature. Rules themselves must be acquired by contingency-shaping, or else the rules would not be obeyed. Driver education begins with rule learning, proceeds to contingency-control expressed as skilful driving, and continues as rule-governed when a driver stops at a red light at a deserted intersection.

Rules are learned from parents, peers, teachers, and religious leaders (these are all significant others, in Sullivan's language, at different stages of development) acting as generalized conditioned reinforcers. Contingency-shaping need not occur first. The child is instructed not to covet or commit adultery long before it knows the meaning of either word. Maybe not the word, Freudians might riposte, but what of the intention? What Freud attributes to 'the unconscious' is unverbalized contingency-shaped behaviour. To bring the unconscious into consciousness, Freud pronounced, is to connect verbal behaviour to motor. Finding exactly the right verbal behaviour is the crux of the clinician's skill.[20]

6

The Unconscious after Freud

Skinner's analysis of verbal behaviour makes his brand of behaviourism as radically different from Watson's as Sullivan's psychodynamics is from Freud's. And just as the Freudian empire has not declined or fallen,[1] so behaviourism is alive and well.

'Behaviourism,' said Mace,[2] 'is dead.' Echoed Burt[3] five years later: '... behaviourism, both in its original or "naive" form and in its later or "sophisticated" forms ..., has proved untenable.' Burt goes on: '... as a basis for a general theory of human experience it is hopelessly inadequate. The need to reintroduce the concept of consciousness seems inescapable.' The operant analysis of verbal behaviour accepts that challenge.

If consciousness is amenable to operant analysis, what about the unconscious? The expurgation of the conscious mind from the lexicon of psychology carries with it the expulsion of the unconscious mind as well, if we are thinking of mind as an object. But if the objection to mind is that behaviour is not entirely controlled by consciousness, then the less control possessed by consciousness, the more must be under unconscious control. In accepting this, the radical behaviourist is in alliance with the psychoanalyst.

Appeals to unconscious forces as controllers of human behaviour are typically made in the special circumstances met in clinical practice, circumstances in which an individual cannot account for certain disturbing activities. In this respect, the peculiar value of the concept of the unconscious is in providing a way of understanding behaviour that is unpredictable and out of control from the point of view of normal consciousness. It places a limitation on the value of consciousness in a psychology concerned with *the prediction and control of behaviour*, but the emphasis of this limitation is on behaviour that is not normal. When Freud extended the coverage of the unconscious beyond the confines of the clinic, he did so in respect of the *psychopathology* of everyday life, and the unconscious has come to acquire a particular quality with which the experimentalist is not supposed to be concerned.

In its earliest days, behaviourism was a repudiation of a psychological orthodoxy dominated by structuralism and the method of introspection, and this purgative side of the system has been principally responsible for the pronouncements of its death. Yet, in the opening sentences of his 1914 text, Watson[4] stated the positive programme of behaviourism starkly and simply as 'the prediction and control of behaviour', and set out to substantiate this programme by discarding consciousness altogether, instead of adding to it as had Freud. Watson had neither the conceptual nor the technical means to put this programme into effect, but these deficiencies have since been remedied by Skinner.

Behaviour is controlled by the reinforcement history of an organism. A chimpanzee will pull a chain 120,000 times before gaining a piece of food. The other 119,999 responses do not make sense to an observer unaware of the animal's reinforcement history.[5] When a lower organism responds according to a particular reinforcement schedule, it is not possible to ask the animal why it behaves as it does, so that control over its behaviour can be attributed to a history of reinforcement without obfuscation by a contemporary verbal explanation. When a human engages in a similar activity, however, such an enquiry is possible and is normally accepted – unless the behaviour is clinically significant, like compulsive handwashing. The significance of neurotic behaviour is that patients (like the chimpanzee) are unable to give a contemporary account of their 'symptoms', and refer to them as beyond their (conscious) control. In these circumstances, Freud popularized the concept of the dynamic unconscious by claiming to demonstrate historical sources of control.

The question of the unconscious, then, reduces to a consideration of historical and contemporary stimulus control of behaviour, and to the correspondence between verbal behaviour and action. Because the neurotic cannot give an acceptable account of his or her contemporary behaviour, attention is directed to its historical origins; because a normal individual does give such an account, attention is drawn to the alleged contemporary controlling factors. In the first case behaviour is thought to depend on unconscious processes, in the second on conscious ones.

To the radical behaviourist, except for rule-governed behaviour, which is explicitly verbal in origin, all activity is unconsciously controlled. It depends upon the history of reinforcement of the activity, and whatever verbal behaviour serves to justify the activity is acquired through an independent reinforcement history of its own. Freud's mechanism of rationalization and other defences of the ego refer to similar states of affairs.

Psychotherapy from the standpoint of a behaviourist

The title of this section is a parody on J.B. Watson's *Psychology from the Standpoint of a Behaviourist*. The parody is not original. It was used by Joel Greenberg and Aaron Bernstein in 1967, and by C.B. Ferster in 1979, both times to illustrate the role of verbal stimuli in behaviour therapy and modification. Thus, although the behaviour therapies of the schools of Eysenck and Wolpe are direct assaults on unacceptable behaviours by conditioning procedures, these procedures can be employed in 'talking cures' (actually listening cures) just as they are in traditional dynamic psychotherapies. The difference is that in psychoanalysis, associations are supposed to be free, while in behavioural therapy, associations are specifically controlled. Therapist training in psychoanalysis indoctrinates the trainee with the theoretical system of the master; in behaviour analysis the trainee learns to be a listener. By listening, however, the behaviour analyst is not aiming to make interpretations of patients' psychodynamics but to teach them to monitor the stimulus control of their behaviour. In behaviour therapy, the therapist controls the stimulus.

Free association is really a contradiction in terms, because its purpose as a therapeutic tool is to lead to the origin of a neurosis. Free association is not free in the sense of 'free will'; it does not mean that the association of ideas is uncontrolled, but that the therapist should not take part in controlling it. After Breuer's case of Anna O, in which hypnosis was used to dictate the therapeutic process, the ideal psychodynamic procedure is to allow the patient's associations to follow their own course to the point of onset of

neurotic behaviour. This is a diagnostic, not a therapeutic, procedure, but as the discovery of the origin of a neurosis is supposed to
be its cure, diagnosis and therapy become essentially one. On this
point there is an affinity between psychoanalysis and behaviour
analysis inasmuch as the extinction of any behaviour can happen
only if the behaviour occurs but its usual consequence does not
follow.

Psychoanalytic therapy is 'interminable', to borrow from Freud,
because it is indifferent to the scientific principles of stimulus-
stimulus association (association of events) and stimulus-response
association (stimulus control of behaviour) that might facilitate its
progress. Behaviour therapy and behaviour modification are
founded explicitly on laboratory discoveries of these principles.
Skilful psychodynamic therapists discover them directly in clinical
practice. Thereafter such therapists prove their insights by interpretation of their patients' unconscious memories. Behaviour
analysts deny the existence of forgotten memories stored in the
unconscious mind and appeal instead to environmental contingencies in explaining the origination and maintenance of symptoms.
Insofar as such symptoms are not under conscious control they can
be attributed to what we can call the radical unconscious, which is
an interpersonal rather than an intrapsychic mechanism.

Behaviour therapy and behaviour modification

I have divided behavioural therapies into behaviour therapy and
behaviour modification, because they derive from different research
traditions: respondent conditioning (see Chapter 4) in the case of
behaviour therapy and operant conditioning (see Chapter 5) in the
case of behaviour modification, and because they employ different
models of behaviour change. Nevertheless behaviour therapy and
behaviour modification both employ a common set of basic terms:
acquisition, extinction, generalization and *discrimination*, all of
which describe relations between responses (segments of behaviour) and stimuli (segments of the environment). Acquisition is the
introduction of a response into an individual's repertoire, extinction
is the elimination of a response from the repertoire, and generalization and discrimination define the range and modalities of
stimuli that elicit a response. Altogether, these are applied to

response substitution, where an acceptable response is substituted for a 'symptom', and stimulus substitution, where a response to an inappropriate stimulus is transferred to an appropriate one.

In *The Causes and Cures of Neurosis*, Eysenck and Rachman list the following characteristics of behaviour therapy that distinguish it from dynamic psychotherapy:

1. Its theory is consistent and testable.
2. It is experimental, not clinical, in origin.
3. It considers symptoms as unadaptive conditioned responses.
4. Symptoms are signs of faulty learning, not repression.
5. Symptoms are not defence mechanisms.
6. Historical events are irrelevant for treatment.
7. Cures occur through direct treatment of symptoms.
8. Interpretation is irrelevant.
9. Symptom substitution is not inevitable.
10. Personal relations are not essential for cures.

Not all of these are characteristics of behaviour modification. Personal relations, for one, are essential in the training of social skills, and a symptom cannot be permanently removed from a client's repertoire in ignorance of his radical unconscious (schedule of reinforcement that maintains the symptom). In behaviour therapy, psychotherapy from the standpoint of a behaviourist means direct treatment of a symptom, not indirect treatment by way of intrapsychic analysis. 'Cures are achieved by treating the symptom itself', not by 'handling the (unconscious) dynamics' that are its cause, say Eysenck and Rachman in distinguishing behaviour therapy from psychotherapy.[6] This is not, however, a distinguishing criterion between psychotherapy and behaviour modification. In both these cases the discovery of unconscious dynamics is an important therapeutic objective; the difference is that psychotherapy undertakes intrapsychic analysis of a hypothetical mental structure while behavioural analysis seeks the interpersonal transactions that maintain an individual's behaviour. These transactions constitute the radical unconscious programmed through experience between the person and his or her community.

Stimulus control and contingency management[7]

Behaviour modification has two components: stimulus control (or substitution) and contingency management. An example of stimulus substitution recommended as a cure for lovesickness appears in *The Two Noble Kinsmen* by Shakespeare and John Fletcher. For our purposes, the principal characters are Arcite and Palamon (two noble knights from Thebes who fought on the losing side against the king of Athens), Emilia (a noblewoman), a gaoler and his daughter, her wooer, and a doctor.

The knights are imprisoned. They see Emilia in the garden, fall in love with her, and gain their freedom long enough for a winner-takes-all encounter. Palamon loses and is condemned to life imprisonment. Meanwhile, back at the gaol, the gaoler's daughter has a yokel wooer. She, however, loves the noble Palamon, and believing that her love is returned, helps him escape from gaol. He deceives her and she loses her reason. In the following excerpt, the doctor proposes to cure her by substituting the wooer for the knight.

The following action comes from Act IV, Scene iii. It is preceded by a sequence in which the doctor is introduced to the gaoler's lovesick daughter. She is gibbering in her madness from unrequited love.

Gaoler: What do you think of her, sir?

Doctor: I think she has a perturbed mind, which I cannot minister to.

Gaoler: Alas, what then?

Doctor: Understand you she ever affected any man ere she beheld Palamon?

Gaoler: I was once in great hope she had fixed her liking on this gentleman my friend.

Wooer: I did think so too ...

Doctor: ... This you must do: confine her to a place where the light may seem to steal in rather than be permitted; take upon you, young sir her friend, the name of Palamon; say you come to eat with her and to commune of love. This will catch her attention, for this her mind beats upon; other objects that are inserted 'tween her mind and eye become the pranks and friskins of her madness. Sing to her such green songs of love as she says Palamon hath sung ... It is a falsehood she is in, which is with falsehoods to be combated ... .

The imitation Palamon secures the maiden's affection. In the second scene of Act V, the doctor, the gaoler, and the wooer disguised as Palamon occupy the stage:

Doctor:
    Has this advice I told you done any good upon her?
Wooer:
    O, very much. The maids that kept her company
    Have half persuaded her that I am Palamon;
    Within this half hour she came smiling to me,
    And asked me what I would eat, and when I would kiss her.
    I told her, presently, and kissed her twice.
Doctor:
    'Twas well done; twenty times had been far better,
    For there the cure lies mainly.

And cured she was. Two scenes later, the real Palamon, on his way to (commuted) execution, learned from the gaoler about his daughter:

Palamon:
    Your gentle daughter gave me freedom once.
    Pray how does she? I heard she was not well
Gaoler:
    Sir she's well restored
    And to be married shortly.

Contingency management is the management of the consequences of specified behaviours. This also was anticipated on the stage, where the most dramatic classical illustration of its use is in Aristophanes' *Lysistrata*. Lysistrata may not have been the first to put contingency management to practical use, but she certainly used it creatively.

'Until', she organized Greek women to say, 'you Greek men abstain from making war, we Greek women will abstain from making love.' With some difficulty she extracted from them the following oath, sworn on a sacrificial bowl of wine:

        I will have nothing to do with my husband or my lover
        Though he come to me in pitiable condition.
        In my house I will be untouchable

In my thinnest saffron silk
And make him long for me.
I will not give myself,
And if he constrains me I will be cold
As ice and never move.
I will not lift my slippers to the ceiling,
Or crouch on all fours like the lioness in the carving.
And if I keep this oath, let me drink from this bowl;
If not, let my bowl be filled with water.[8]

The power to affect consequences is a necessary prerequisite of contingency management; the manager must have something to withhold.[9] Lysistrata had a natural advantage in this respect, but not all the power was in her hands. She could not force the ladies of Greece to agree to her conditions, and some small signs of a female rebellion were written into the play. And the warriors, had Mars been ready for the rape of Venus, might have taken their lovesickness to another venue. Maupassant describes the Lysistrata situation in a short story (variously translated as 'A Crisis' and 'In the Bedroom') in which a wife 'contingency manages' her adulterous husband by denying him free access to her bedroom.

I give these literary examples of contingency management not to illustrate the priority of art over science but to suggest why psychoanalysis predominates over behaviour analysis in the public mind. First of all, of course, is Freud's identification with sex as the root of mental illness, but second is his aptitude as a narrator. It was his appeal to the literary more than to the medical community that promoted his ideas. Neither Watson nor Pavlov made anything of literary sources; nor did they employ sexual frustration in their scientific investigations. Nearly always these derived from hungry animals, although there is a reported case of 'experimental neurosis' where impedance of sexual appetite in a dog was involved. The case was reported in the *Pavlovian Journal of Biological Science* by M.M. Khananashvili in 1976:

A female in heat was placed in the experimental room, where conditioned food reflexes were elaborating in the male. The male, as a rule, came to the female and gave no reactions to conditioned stimuli until the end of coitus. Just after that, the conditioned food activity recovered without any declination. But, if the female was isolated with a wire-net so that the male could not copulate, an even short-term sojourning of the female in the experimental room disturbed all the conditioned reflexes in the male. A strongly pronounced neurosis was elicited by a long-term placing of the female in the experimental room ... .

This dog would be a strong candidate for behaviour therapy on Eysenck's and Rachman's terms.

Philosophy and the behaviourists

Despite its scientific grounding, behaviour analysis does not command the popular and intellectual following that psychoanalysis has secured. Probably this is because the Freudian metaphor accords with accepted wisdom while radical behaviourism does not, but a further reason is that in popular and technical expositions behaviourists repeated the kinds of errors that Susan Stebbing attributed to the physicists in *Philosophy and the Physicists*. These mistakes were not to do with the nature of physics as popularly expounded by Eddington and Jeans in the 1930s, but with the way these philosopher-physicists confused technical and real-world languages. It is true, Stebbing noted, that in modern sub-atomic physics there is more space than substance, but the same is not true of the floor on which we walk. To warn the walker of danger in crossing from one room to another as though he were stepping across electrons is a mistaken application of the vocabulary of physics to the vocabulary of everyday life.

Behaviourists may have made the identical error by forcing on the natural language restrictions in vocabulary that apply only to technical psychology. Thus in *Beyond Freedom and Dignity*, Skinner explained behaviourism to the wider community in ordinary language, forgetting that verbal behaviours have different reinforcement histories in the general and scientific populations. He denied humans freedom and dignity, and of course he was disregarded. By confusing the existential and functional meanings of the words, Skinner copied Eddington's mistake of applying the physicists' concept of space to the space of the ordinary world. Eddington forgot that one space is a micro- and the other is a macro-cosmos, and Skinner forgot that functional freedom is not the same as existential freedom. Personally, the behaviourist is not as mindless as he claims, just as the universe is not expanding in the street.

Psychoanalysts have not made the mistake of the behaviourists although they too remove the control of behaviour from the conscious mind. Freud denied men and women dignity and freedom surreptitiously by attributing their behaviour to an unconscious obsessed with procreation. But, unlike Skinner's, his denial was grafted onto the vocabulary of the existential world. This is because instead of denying what is open to introspection, Freud added something that is beyond it. Psychoanalysis does not compete for terms with the wider world but adds a functional vocabulary (the unconscious mind) to an experiential vocabulary (the conscious mind) already in existence. Ironically, while behaviourism is deadening as a literature, it lives on as a science of behaviour; and while psychoanalysis is dead as a science, its soul goes dramatically marching on.[10]

REQUIEM

And Therefore Never Send to Know

There's nothing simply good, nor ill alone,
Of every quality comparison
The only measure is, and judge, opinion.
  John Donne, *The Progress of the Soul*, First Song, LII

For whom tolls the bell?

As a proem was needed to introduce this book, so a requiem is required to conclude it. It does not have to be massive but I mean it to be substantial. In particular, is it a requiem for the living or an epitaph for the dead? And if the dead, whose corpse?

C.A. Mace announced the death of behaviourism in the year that *Verbal Behavior* was published, and in 1985 H.J. Eysenck documented how the Freudian Empire has fallen into decline.[1] In each of these pronouncements nothing was said but the truth: what was omitted was the whole truth. For behaviourism, as I have indicated, the whole truth is that Skinner's behaviourism is a paradigm away from Watson's dead infant; and there is more to the Freudian Empire than the science that Eysenck mercilessly shovelled into a pauper's grave. Freud, wrote Donald Spence,[2] was not a scientist but a narrator and he surgically cut the Freudian metaphor from the Freudian myth, bringing Freud the Gothic novelist back to life only two years after Eysenck laid Freud the hopeful scientist to rest. 'To keep alive the Freudian metaphor,' Spence wrote,

> – that is the challenge of the moment. To keep it uppermost in our awareness and prevent it from becoming transparent allows us to keep its metaphorical nature clearly in mind, to avoid the trap of

projecting its terms onto the clinical domain and finding things that are really not there.

Breuer recognized the danger of slipping from simile to metaphor in his theoretical contribution to *Studies on Hysteria* with Freud. In a passage on 'hysterical conversion' that comes close to Pavlov on the neural basis of the conditioned reflex, he added in a footnote that he was 'anxious not to drive the analogy with an electrical system to death'. But neither he nor Freud considered that the conversion in hysteria was not from mental to physical but from simile to metaphor.

Freud's misfortune was his training in Victorian European medicine, which locked psychoanalysis into the scientific atomism of the era. Now, we can see psychoanalysis for what it is – a system of 'alternative' or holistic medicine cloaked in a white coat, waving a magic wand. It is the white coat metaphor that needs discarding, not the holism, because the alternative medicine that we now call non-traditional is more true than modern medicine to the Hippocratic tradition, wherein case histories and clinical pictures take precedence over diagnoses and particularized disease entities.[3] Psychoanalysis and behaviour analysis (modification) alike follow in this tradition, behaviour therapy does not.

So, stripped of coat and wand, psychoanalysis may not be ready for the grave. In the light of postmodern hermeneutics, a case for Freud's philosophy can be made.[4] Psychoanalysis lives as a chronic engagement of analysand with analyst; its image as acute mental surgery is dead. That image lives more suitably in the behaviour therapy that Eysenck has described.

As it happens, Eysenck has a unique place in the present discourse. First of all, he is the only one of Freud's rivals in the present company to build his system on formal statistical procedures, and, secondly, he is among the supporters of the rebirth of the cognitive psychology that Watson thought he had put into the ground.[5] Ostensibly burying Watson, Eysenck wrote with S. Rachman in 1965, '... it is becoming more and more widely recognized that between stimulus and response interposes an organism, and the formula S-O-R has pretty well superseded the old S-R paradigm'.[6] The O, of course, is the personality that has long been supposed to determine the unique way in which an individual behaves, but how to make contact with this personality except through the behaviour it determines is never explained. Individuality must be described before it can be explained, and I showed in an earlier chapter how Eysenck arrived at an economically descriptive vocabulary derived from associations (correlations) first between miniature laboratory situations and then between questionnaire responses, but it does not follow that the associations are within the individual (O) or that they serve as explanations any more than do the associations plumbed by Freud or Jung.

Writing of associations (or correlations) in a passage that applies equally to the systems of Eysenck, Pavlov, Freud, Jung, and modern cognitive psychologists in general, Skinner has this to say:

> Take ... the so-called process of association. In Pavlov's experiment a hungry dog hears a bell and is then fed. If this happens many times, the dog begins to salivate when it hears the bell. The standard mentalistic explanation is that the dog 'associates' the bell with the food. But it was Pavlov who associated them! ... The dog merely begins to salivate upon hearing the bell. We have no evidence that it does so because of an internal surrogate of the contingencies (p. 1).[7]

Internal surrogates are the historical subjects of psychology and modern cognitive scientists seek diligently for their neural correlates just as Freud (intrapsychic associations based on personal significance) and Pavlov (interneural associations based on temporal proximity) did originally. But the egocentric paradigm that directed the efforts of these masters has been supplanted by another, and it is this new interpersonal paradigm that I come not to bury but to praise.[8] As for the dead, who now remembers the phlogiston of the chemist or the physicist's ether? How long before the memory silo is forgotten in summoning up remembrance of things past?[9]

Confronted with the remembrance of things to come, we are faced with burying not the dead but the hatchet. In spirit, the intrapsychic and interpersonal paradigms elucidate the opposition of appearance and illusion in the nature of individuality – the oxymoronic status of modern psychology. As Matthew Ahern concludes his poem, 'Oxymoron',[10]

... you must exert two counter forces equally
Forever and thus create a unity based on tension.

Among the master builders of modern psychology, Freud and Skinner tower as twin peaks of this tension. Neither the appearance nor the illusion of personality is ready for burial yet. If a metaphor we have to have, it is the Easter one of rising from the dead, and the expression of this metaphor that most befits this book is the lamentation of the failed suicide in the novel, *Ever After*: 'I am not me. Therefore was I ever me? That is the gist of it.'[11] Freud was not what he made himself out to be, and he was not the beginning of an era, but the end of one.[12] Skinner is not what he has been made out to be, and he is not the end of an era, but the beginning.[13] And the physical science catchphrase for this new era is 'dynamical systems', a catchphrase that Harry Stack Sullivan could have used. Social scientists also have shoulders to climb on, given a little help from their friends.

Notes

Preface

1. Timothy Findley, *Headhunter*, Toronto: Harper Collins, 1993, p. 239.

2. A different kind of paradigm shift, to cognitive from behavioural and psychoanalytic psychology, has been debated. See E.M. Segal & R. Lachman, 'Complex behavior or higher mental processes: is there a paradigm shift?' *American Psychologist*, 1972, **27**, 46-55. The present change is like the change in the physical sciences occasioned by chaos theory. Like chaos, transactions in psychology stem not from linear but from non-linear relationships of the form 'A is a function of B is a function of A ...'.

3. For a thoughtful discussion of the place of history and systems in the teaching of psychology, see John J. Furedy, 'The Socratic-Sophistic continuum in teaching psychology and psychological research in America', in A.E. Puente, J.R. Matthews, & C.L. Brewer, *Teaching Psychology in America: A History*, Washington: American Psychological Association, 1992. For a thoughtful reconstruction of 'historical origins of psychological research' in a transactional paradigm see Kurt Danziger, *Constructing the Subject*, Cambridge: Cambridge University Press, 1990. Danziger concludes that historically, 'the work of psychologists represented a kind of celebration of the myth of the independent individual in its pure form' and describes this, elegantly, as the Robinson Crusoe myth.

Proem: On mind and behaviour

1. J. Dewey & A.F. Bentley, *Knowing and the Known*, Boston: Beacon Press, 1949.

2. See T.S. Kuhn, *The Structure of Scientific Revolutions*, Chicago: University of Chicago Press, 1962, for an account of paradigms in science.

3. See above, Preface, note 2.

4. Eric Berne's *Transactional Analysis in Psychotherapy*, New York: Grove Press, 1961, is an explicit extension of psychoanalysis into this paradigm. He presents in popular form several 'pathological' interpersonal transactions in *Games People Play*, New York: Grove Press, 1964. The paradigm also encloses Gestalt psychology, which refutes atomism with the assertion that the whole is greater than the sum of its parts. Typically, Gestalt principles are buttressed by perceptual demonstrations, such as reversible figures where the same 'parts' can appear in different forms, but the principles also apply to interpersonal transactions, where the relationship is more than the characters of the individual participants. See also H. Cantril, A. Ames, A.H. Hastorff, & W.H. Ittelson, 'Psychology and scientific research III. The transactional view in psychological research', *Science*, 1949, **110**, 517-22.

5. For brief accounts of the beginnings of contemporary psychology, see F.S. Keller, *The Definition of Psychology*, New York: Appleton-Century-Crofts, 1973 (2nd ed.), and W.M. O'Neil, *The Beginnings of Modern Psychology*, Harmondsworth: Penguin, 1968.

6. As a theoretician, Skinner was preceded by J.R. Kantor, but Kantor did not engage in laboratory work. See J.R. Kantor & N.W. Smith, *The Science of Psychology: An Interbehavioral Survey*. Chicago: Principia Press, 1975, for an overview of Kantor's theoretical system. A detailed point-by-point comparison of Skinner's and Kantor's systems appears in E.K. Morris, 'Some relationships between interbehavioral psychology and radical behaviorism', *Behaviorism*, 1982, **10**, 187-216.

7. This double holism is expressed existentially in Chapter 2 as 'being-in the world'.

8. For an original different view of this separation see Julian Jaynes, *The Origin of Consciousness in the Breakdown of the Bicameral Mind*, Boston: Houghton Mifflin, 1977.

9. As late as 1931 Kurt Lewin complained that psychology was still in the pre-modern mode of science. See K. Lewin, 'The conflict between Aristotelian and Galileian modes of thought in contemporary psychology', *Journal of General Psychology*, 1931, **5**, 141-77. Reprinted as ch. 1 in his *A Dynamic Theory of Personality*, New York: McGraw Hill, 1935.

10. See R.S. Woodworth. 'Four varieties of behaviorism', *Psychological Review*, 1924, **31**, 257-64. For later accounts of varieties of behaviourism see V.L. Lee, *Beyond Behaviorism*, Hillsdale: Erlbaum, 1988, and G.E. Zuriff, *Behaviorism: A Conceptual Reconstruction*, New York: Columbia University Press, 1985.

1. Freudian Psychodynamics

1. See J.W. Barron, M.N. Eagle, & D.L. Wolitzky (eds.), *Interface of Psychoanalysis and Psychology*, Washington: American Psychological Association, 1992. An alliance with behaviourism is also promised in this book, indexed as behaviourism, integrated with psychoanalytic theory, but the indexed page is blank. In the present work I hope to rectify this omission.

2. See *The Psychopathology of Everyday Life*, first published in 1901. For a modern experimental attack on some of these phenomena, including hypnosis, see E.R. Hilgard, Divided *Consciousness: Multiple Controls in Human Thought and Action*, New York: Wiley, 1977.

3. There were other references to unconscious mentality before Freud. See L.L. Whyte, The *Unconscious before Freud*, Basic Books, 1960, and H.F. Ellenberger, *The Discovery of the Unconscious*, New York: Basic Books, 1970. A series of papers reappraising the unconscious appear in K.S. Bowers & D. Meichenbaum (eds.), *The Unconscious: A Reappraisal*, New York: Wiley, 1984.

4. H. Hartmann, 'Technical implications of ego psychology', *Psychoanalytic Quarterly*, 1951, **20**, 31-43.

5. See Ernest Jones, *The Life and Work of Sigmund Freud*, New York: Basic Books, vol. 1 1953, vol. 2 1955, vol. 3 1957.

6. M.M. Gill, 'Psychoanalysis and exploratory psychotherapy', *Journal of the American Psychoanalytic Association*, 1954, **2**, 771-9. Italics added.

7. S. Freud, 'On the history of the psychoanalytic movement', *Collected Papers*, vol. 1, London: Hogarth, 1924, p. 287. Italics added.

8. At this point I write 'hysteria' to acknowledge the varying meanings of this label throughout medical history. See Helen King, 'Once upon a text', in S. Gilman, H. King, R. Porter, & E. Showalter, *Hysteria Beyond Freud*, Berkeley: University of California Press, 1993, 3-90.

9. J. Breuer & S. Freud, *Studies on Hysteria*, New York: Basic Books, 1957 (first published 1895). See E.R. Hilgard, *Divided Consciousness*, for non-Freudian examples of therapy by hypnosis, and H. Ellenberger, 'The Story of Anna O: a critical review with new data', *History of the Behavioral Sciences*, 1972, **8**, 267-9, for another look at the case of Anna O, where catharsis and symptom removal were first described by Breuer.

10. S. Freud, 'Repression', *Collected Papers*, vol. 4, London: Hogarth, 1925.

11. J.D. Keehn, 'Experimental studies of "the unconscious"', *Behavior Research and Therapy*, 1967, **5**, 95-102; R.F. Hefferline & B. Keenan, 'Amplitude-induction gradient of a small-scale (covert) operant', *Journal of the Experimental Analysis of Behavior*, 1963, **6**, 307-15.

12. J.B. Watson held a similar view: see 'The unconscious of the behaviorist', in M. Prince (ed.) *The Unconscious: A Symposium*, New York: Knopf, 1928.

13. S. Freud, *The Ego and the Id*, New York: Norton, 1962, p. 20 (first published 1923).

14. S. Freud, *The Ego and the Id*, p. 23.

15. H. Hartmann, 'Comments on the psychoanalytic theory of the ego', *Psychoanalytic Study of the Child*, 1950, **5**, 74-96; and 'Ego psychology and the problem of adaptation', in D. Rappaport (ed.), *Organization and Pathology of Thought*, New York: Columbia University Press, 1951.

16. See H. Hartmann (note 4) and M.M. Gill, 'Ego psychology and psychotherapy', *Psychoanalytic Quarterly*, 1951, **20**, 62-71.

17. S. Freud, 'On narcissism: an introduction', *Collected Papers*, vol. 4, London: Hogarth, 1925.

18. For a full account of the defence mechanisms, see Anna Freud, *The Ego and the Mechanisms of Defense*, New York: International Universities Press, 1946 (first published in 1936).

19. S. Freud, 'Repression', *Collected Papers*, vol. 4, 1925.

20. S. Freud, 'Instincts and their vicissitudes', *Collected Papers*, vol. 4. 1925.

21. Anna Freud, 'Symposium on genetic psychology. 2. The contribution of psychoanalysis to genetic psychology', *American Journal of Orthopsychiatry*, 1951, **21**, 476-97.

22. R. Schafer, 'Regression in the service of the ego: the relevance of a psychoanalytic concept for personality assessment', in G. Lindzey (ed.), *Assessment of Human Motives*. New York: Rinehart, 1958.

23. For some non-psychoanalytic critiques of this linkage see J.D. Keehn (ed.), *Creativity and Madness: An Interdisciplinary Symposium*, North York, Ontario: Captus Press, 1987; A. Rothenberg, *Creativity and Madness: New Findings and Old Stereotypes*, Baltimore: Johns Hopkins University Press, 1990; K.R. Jamison, *Touched with Fire*, New York: Free Press.

24. B.I. Murstein & R.S. Pryer, 'The concept of projection: a review', *Psychological Bulletin*, 1959, **56**, 353-74.

25. J.H. Van den Berg, *The Phenomenological Approach to Psychiatry*, Springfield, Ill.: Thomas, 1955.

26. O.H. Mowrer, *Learning Theory and Personality Dynamics*, New York: Ronald, 1950. For a later account of Mowrer's views see 'New evidence concerning the nature of psychopathology', in M.J. Feldman (ed.), *Studies in Psychotherapy and Behavioral Change*, Buffalo: University of Buffalo Press, 1968.

27. Karl Menninger, *Theory of Psychoanalytic Technique*, New York: Basic Books, 1958.

28. See Anna Freud, *The Ego and the Mechanisms of Defence*, and S. Freud, 'Analysis terminable and interminable', *Collected Papers*, vol. 5, London: Hogarth, 1957.

29. Repetition compulsion was introduced by Freud after World War I to supplant the autonomy of the pleasure principle and wish fulfilment theory of dreams on account of evidence of repetitive nightmares experienced by many soldiers. S. Freud, *Beyond the Pleasure Principle*, Standard Edition, vol. 18, London: Hogarth, 1955,

30. A. Ellis, 'There is no place for sin in the concept of psychotherapy', *Journal of Counselling Psychology*, 1960, **7**, 188-92.

31. S. Freud, *A General Introduction to Psychoanalysis*, London: Allen and Unwin, 1922.

32. S. Freud, 'Character and anal eroticism', *Collected Papers*, vol. 2, London: Hogarth, 1924.

33. K. Abraham, 'The first pregenital state of the libido', in *Selected Papers*, London: Hogarth, 1916.

34. E. Glover, 'Notes on oral character-formation', *International Journal of Psychoanalysis*, 1925, **6**, 131-53.

35. O. Rank, *The Trauma of Birth*, New York: Harcourt Brace, 1929.

36. S.R. Pinneau, 'The infantile disorders of hospitalism and anaclitic depression', *Psychological Bulletin*, **52**, 429-52.

37. H.F. Harlow, 'Love in infant monkeys', *Scientific American*, 1959, **200**, 68-74; H.F. Harlow & R.R. Zimmermann, 'Affectional responses in the infant monkey', *Science*, 1959, **130**, 421-32.

38. S.J. Suomi & H.F. Harlow, 'Social rehabilitation of isolation-reared monkeys', *Developmental Psychology*, 1972, **6**, 487-92. See also J.D. Keehn, *Animal Models for Psychiatry*, London: Routledge and Kegan Paul, 1986, for a brief review of effects of maternal deprivation in different species.

39. F. Goldman, 'Breast feeding and character formation', *Journal of Personality*, 1948, **17**, 83-103; and 1950, **19**, 189-96.

40. Susan Isaacs, *Social Development in Young Children*, London: Routledge, 1933.

41. E. Fromm, *Fear of Freedom*, London: Routledge & Kegan Paul, 1942.

42. M. Klein, *The Psychoanalysis of Children*, London: Hogarth, 1963.

43. B. Malinowski, *Sex and Repression in Savage Society*, New York: Humanities Press, 1927.

44. Psychological science is not a monolithic edifice. See J. Beloff, *Psychological Sciences: A Review of Modern Psychology*, London: Crosby, Lockwood, Staples, 1973; J.D. Keehn, *The Prediction and Control of Behavior*, Beirut: Khayat, 1962. For a more general account of different sciences, see A.W. Halpin, 'James Clerk Maxwell on the dynamical and statistical modes of thought about men', *Journal of Abnormal Psychology*, 1951, **46**, 257.

45. M. Krull, *Freud and his Father* (A.J. Pomerans, trans.), London: Hutchinson, 1986; J.M. Masson, *Freud: The Assault on Truth: Freud's Suppression of the*

Seduction Theory, New York: Farrar, Straus and Giroux, 1984; E.M. Thornton, *The Freudian Fallacy*, New York: Doubleday, 1984.

46. Reliability is not a salient characteristic of Freud's reporting. For both his interpretation of the case of Little Hans and the personality of Leonardo da Vinci he relied on inaccurate data. See J. Wolpe and S. Rachman, 'Psychoanalytic evidence: a critique based on the case of Little Hans', and B. Farrell, 'On Freud's study of Leonardo', in M. Philipson (ed.), *Leonardo da Vinci: Aspects of the Renaissance Genius*, New York: Braziller, 1966, 224-75. Figure 70 in this book shows the original drawing that Freud did not use. Farrell gives the history of Freud's incredible error in his footnote 8.

47. For a sustained attack on psychoanalysis as a scientific theory see H.J. Eysenck, *The Decline and Fall of the Freudian Empire*, New York: Viking Press, 1985. For criticism of psychoanalysis as a scientific therapy, see Anthony Storr, 'Why psychoanalysis is not a science', in M.C. Blakemore (ed.), *Mind-waves*, Oxford: Blackwell, 1987.

48. F.C. Bartlett, *Remembering*, Cambridge: Cambridge University Press, 1932.

49. See H.L. Roediger III, 'Implicit memory: retention without remembering', *American Psychologist*, 1990, **45**, 1043-56, for a review of recent research on implicit and explicit remembering.

50. D.O. Hebb, 'Science and the world of imagination', *Canadian Psychological Review*, 1975, **16**, 4-11, argues for the place of imagination in science. The mark of a creative scientist, he argues, is the ability to employ data imaginatively, not exhaustively. Science, he argues, requires judgement as well as objectivity.

51. See Anthony Storr, 'Why psychoanalysis is not a science'.

52. See J. Berman, *The Talking Cure: Literary Representations of Psychoanalysis*, New York: New York University Press, 1985; E. Kurtweil and W. Phillips (eds.), *Literature and Psychoanalysis*, New York: Columbia University Press, 1983.

53. B.F. Skinner, *Contingencies of Reinforcement*, New York: Appleton-Century-Crofts, 1969.

2. Rivals to the Personality Model

1. C.G. Jung, *Modern Man in Search of a Soul*, New York: Harcourt Brace, 1933, 182.

2. C.G. Jung, *Modern Man*, 180.

3. See C.G. Jung, *Studies in Word Association*, London: Routledge & Kegan Paul, 1918. Jung, like Freud, subscribed to the classical psychological doctrine of associationism, but Jung's use of associations was by the controlled method – he provided the stimulus, the patient supplied the associated response. In Freud's case, associations were free – the patient provided both stimulus and response.

4. Freud learned his psychology of women from his clinical practice; Jung learned it from James Joyce. Writing to Joyce about *Ulysses* in August, 1932, Jung said: 'The 40 pages of non stop run in the end is a string of veritable psychological peaches. I suppose the devil's grandmother knows so much about the real psychology of a woman. I didn't.' From Richard Ellman (ed.), *The Collected Letters of James Joyce*, vol. 3, New York: Viking Press, 1966, 253.

5. C.G. Jung, *Modern Man*, 86.

6. K. Lewin, 'The conflict between Aristotelian and Galileian modes of thought in contemporary psychology', *Journal of General Psychology*, 1931, **5**, 141-77.

7. C.G. Jung, *Modern Man*, 93.

8. Anthony Stevens, *On Jung*, London: Routledge, 1990, characterizes Jung's own career in this framework. A similar framework is employed by Virginia Woolf in following six lifespans in *The Waves*. See Lyndall Gordon's chapter, 'Speciman Lives', in *Virginia Woolf: A Writer's Life*, Oxford: Oxford University Press, 1984.

9. H.J. Eysenck, 'The conditioning model of neurosis', *Behavioral and Brain Sciences*, 1979, **2**, 155-99.

10. See H.J. Eysenck, *Decline and Fall of the Freudian Empire*, New York: Viking, 1985.

11. W. McDougall, *An Introduction to Social Psychology*, (26th ed.) London: Methuen, 1945, 25.

12. Personality structures based on factor analysis are not a monopoly of the London school. For a broad overview of the current situation, which is a debate over the validity of a five-factor structure, see L.R. Goldberg, 'The structure of phenotypic personality traits', *American Psychologist*, 1993, **48**, 26-33.

13. H.J. Eysenck & S. Rachman, *The Causes and Cures of Neurosis*, San Diego: Knapp, 1965.

14. H.J. Eysenck, 'The conditioning model of neurosis', 155.

15. H.J. Eysenck, ibid., 159.

16. See G.W Allport, *Becoming: Basic Considerations for a Psychology of Personality*, New Haven: Yale University Press, 1955.

17. M. Boss, *Psychoanalysis and Daseinsanalysis* (Ludwig B. Lefebre, trans.), New York: Basic Books, 1963.

18. Ibid., 33.

19. Ibid., 43, italics added.

20. Ibid., 45.

21. J.H. Van den Berg, *A Phenomenological Approach to Psychiatry*, Springfield, Ill: Thomas, 1955.

22. Ibid., 35. Italics in original.

23. M. Boss, *Psychoanalysis and Daseinsanalysis*, 142.

24. For a confluence of existential and behavioural metapsychologies, see S. Krale & C.E. Grenness, 'Skinner and Sartre: towards a radical phenomenology of behavior?', *Review of Existential Psychology and Psychiatry*, 1967, **7**, 128-48. With respect to the inseparability of man and the world he inhabits, see J.R. Kantor, 'Preface to interbehavioral psychology', *Psychological Record*, 1942, **5**, 173-93.

25. E. Weigert, 'Existentialism and its relation to psychotherapy', *Psychiatry*, 1949, **12**, 399-412.

26. Ibid.

3. Rivals to the Personality Paradigm

1. Marianne Krull claims that Freud renounced the seduction theory to save accusing his own father of perversion. This was on account of Freud's self-analysis, not analysis of his patients. See M. Krull, *Freud and his Father* (A.J. Pomerans, trans.), London: Hutchinson, 1986.

2. E. Jones, *The Life and Work of Sigmund Freud*, New York: Basic Books, 1955 (abridged edition, L. Trilling & S. Marcus, eds.), 315.

3. Ibid., 315.

4. See G.W. Allport, *Personality: A Psychological Interpretation*, New York: Holt, 1937; G.W. Allport, 'The general and the unique in psychological science',

Journal of Personality, 1962, **30**, 405-22.

5. H.L. Ansbacher, Causality and indeterminism according to Alfred Adler and some current American personality theories', in K.A. Adler & D. Deutsch (eds.), *Essays in Individual Psychology: Contemporary Applications of Alfred Adler's Theories*, New York: Grove Press, 1959.

6. Adler's clinical psychiatry agrees with Allport's academic psychology on a number of points including the idiographic approach, the uniqueness of the individual, the determination of behaviour by future goals and the centrality of some traits as compared to others. See G.W. Allport, *Becoming*, New Haven: Yale University Press, 1955.

7. In reinforcement terms, the mother's failure to reinforce the child's behaviour, either by neglect or by active opposition, could heighten feelings of failure and, at the same time, weaken the mother, and by generalization, other people, as social reinforcers.

8. See G.R. Patterson & J.B. Reid, 'Reciprocity and coercion: two facets of social systems', in C. Neuringer & J.L. Michael (eds.), *Behavior Modification in Clinical Psychology*, New York: Appleton-Century-Crofts, 1970.

9. As Ullman and Krasner put it, 'Abnormal behavior is no different from normal behavior in its development, its maintenance, or the manner in which it may eventually be changed ... The principles of the development of "proper" beliefs are the same as the principles of the development of "false" beliefs.' L.P. Ullman & L. Krasner, *A Psychological Approach to Abnormal Behavior*, Englewood Cliffs, N.J.: Prentice-Hall, 1969, 92.

10. A. Adler, *The Problem Child*, New York: Capricorn, 1963 (first German edition, 1930).

11. For a behavioural account of how to go about this, see C.B. Ferster, 'Psychotherapy from the standpoint of a behaviorist', in J.D. Keehn (ed.), *Psychopathology in Animals: Research and Clinical Implications*, New York: Academic Press, 1979.

12. H.S. Sullivan, 'The illusion of personal individuality', *Psychiatry*, 1950, **13**, 317-32.

13. B.F. Skinner, *Verbal Behavior*, New York: Appleton-Century-Crofts, 1957.

14. J.R. Kantor & N.W. Smith, *The Science of Psychology: An Interbehavioral Survey*, Chicago: Principia Press, 1975.

15. H.S. Sullivan. *Conceptions of Modern Psychiatry*, Washington: William Alanson White Foundation, 1947, vi.

16. Sullivan's definition of personality makes it the equivalent of an attractor in modern chaos theory. To paraphrase J. Gleich (*Chaos: Making a New Science*, London: Penguin, 1987), personality may be defined as 'the trajectory of an individual dynamical system towards which all other trajectories of the individual's behaviour converge'. See also S. Barton, 'Chaos, self-organization, and psychology', *American Psychologist*, 1994, **49**, 5-14.

17. H.S. Sullivan, *Conceptions of Modern Psychiatry*, vi.

18. H.S. Sullivan, *The Interpersonal Theory of Psychiatry*, New York: Norton, 1953, 159.

19. H.S. Sullivan, *Conceptions of Modern Psychiatry*, 9.

20. Particularly Clark Hull and his followers. See C.L. Hull, *Principles of Behavior*, New York: Appleton-Century, 1943.

21. H.S. Sullivan, *Interpersonal Theory*, 164.

22. Ibid., 158

23. For laboratory examples of conditioning without awareness, see J.D. Keehn, 'Experimental studies of "the unconscious": operant conditioning of unconscious eyeblinking', *Behavior Research and Therapy*, 1967, **5**, 95-102.

24. B.F. Skinner, *Science & Human Behavior*, New York: MacMillan, 1953.

25. B.F. Skinner, *Verbal Behavior*, New York: Appleton-Century-Crofts, 1957.

26. H.S. Sullivan, *Interpersonal Theory*, 103.

27. From A.W. Combs & D. Snygg, *Individual Behavior: A Perceptual Approach to Behavior*, New York: Harper, 1959, 21-2.

28. This is what Skinner calls superstitious behaviour. See B.F. Skinner, ' "Superstition" in the pigeon', *Journal of Experimental Psychology*, 1948, **38**, 168-72.

29. H.S. Sullivan. *Interpersonal Theory*, 184.

30. Not all students of animal learning hold this view, or even all behaviourists. An early cognitive account of animal learning was advanced by W. Kohler in *The Mentality of Apes*, New York: Harcourt Brace, 1925. A cognitive-type view was also championed by the behaviourist E.C. Tolman in *Purposive Behavior in Animals & Men*, New York: Appleton-Century, 1932.

31. See J.D. Keehn, 'Consciousness and the stimulus control of behavior', in R.M. Gilbert & N.S. Sutherland (eds.), *Animal Discrimination Learning*, New York: Academic Press, 1969.

32. C. Spearman, *Abilities of Man*, London: Macmillan, 1927.

33. H.S. Sullivan, *Interpersonal Theory*, 6.

34. Sullivan often refers to the mothering-one to allow for the contingency that the nursing person may not be the natural mother.

35. H.S. Sullivan, *Interpersonal Theory*, 72.

36. Ibid., 72.

37. C.B. Ferster & B.F. Skinner, *Schedules of Reinforcement*, New York: Appleton-Century-Crofts, 1957.

38. B.F. Skinner, ' "Superstition" in the pigeon', *Journal of Experimental Psychology*, 1948, **38**, 168-72.

39. See H.S. Sullivan, 'The illusion of personal individuality'.

40. H.S. Sullivan, *Interpersonal Theory*, 190.

41. Ibid., 191.

42. See D.J. Levis, 'The infrahuman avoidance model of symptom maintenance and implosive therapy', in J.D. Keehn (ed.), *Psychopathology in Animals*, 257-77.

43. H.S. Sullivan, *Interpersonal Theory*, 198.

44. Ibid., 193 (italics in original).

45. Ibid., 230.

46. Ibid., 262.

47. Ibid., 297.

4. Respondent Conditioning: Pavlov

1. For a brief history of conditioning see M.R. Rosensweig's papers, 'Salivary conditioning before Pavlov', *American Journal of Psychology*, 1959, **72**, 628-33, and 'Pavlov, Bechterev and Twitmyer on conditioning', *American Journal of Psychology*, 1960, **73**, 312-16. See also K.M. Dallenbach's paper 'Twitmyer and the conditioned response', *American Journal of Psychology*, 1959, **72**, 633-8.

2. The fact was also known to Guy de Maupassant, who vividly described a case of associated stimuli in a short story called 'A Vendetta (or Semillante)' in which an old widow trains her dog to savage the murderer of her son. See Guy de Maupassant, *The Complete Short Stories*, New York: Doubleday, Hanover House, 1955. Oliver Wendell Holmes Sr. also imagined conditioning in a novel first published in 1885, See his *A Moral Antipathy*, Boston: Houghton Mifflin, 1887, for an account of a child's fear conditioned to the sight of the girl who had dropped him.

3. Why, you might ask, was Shaw so anti-Pavlov? There are two reasons: First, he was an anti-vivisectionist, and secondly, he was miffed by a remark of H.G. Wells that if Shaw and Pavlov were drowning and Wells had only one lifebelt he would throw it to the more important one for humanity – Pavlov.

4. I.P. Pavlov, *Conditioned Reflexes: An Investigation of the Physiological Activity of the Cerebral Cortex* (G.V. Anrep, trans.), Oxford: Oxford University Press, 1927, 6.

5. I.P. Pavlov, *Conditioned Reflexes*, 17-18.

6. Once it acquires the power to reinforce in the absence of the US, the CS acts as a surrogate for the US, rather than as a signal. In the first case, the CS prepares the animal to eat; in the second case, the CS acts as if it were food.

7. The relationship between CS and US is not only associative; the CS also signals, or predicts, the US. Consequences of this relationship have been explored by R.A. Rescorla, 'Pavlovian conditioning and its proper control procedures', *Psychological Review*, 1967, **74**, 71-80.

8. I.P. Pavlov, *Conditioned Reflexes*, 90.

9. See Chapter 3, and J.A. Gray, *Pavlov's Typology: Recent Theoretical and Experimental Developments from the Laboratory of B.M. Teplov*, Oxford: Pergamon, 1964.

10. R.A. Rescorla, 'Second-order conditioning: implications for theories of learning', in F.J. McGuigan and D.B. Lumsden (eds.), *Contemporary Approaches to Conditioning and Learning*, New York: Winston, 1973, offers another view.

11. I.P. Pavlov, *Conditioned Reflexes*, 291.

12. Ibid., 7, italics added.

13. Ibid., 14.

14. Pavlov's objection to the study of the motor component of a UR has already been noted. However it has recently been pointed out that in his contribution to Murchison's *Psychologies of 1930* Pavlov remarked: 'Let us take any natural phenomenon that has never had any relation to food motion or food secretion. If this phenomenon precedes the act of eating ... it will later ... become a surrogate for food – the animal moves toward it and may even take it into its mouth ... See H.M. Jenkins & B.R. Moore, 'The form of the autoshaped response with food or water reinforcers', *Journal of the Experimental Analysis of Behavior*, 1973, **20**, 163-81.

15. See W.J. Brogden, 'Animal studies of learning', in S.S. Stevens (ed.), *Handbook of Experimental Psychology*, New York: Wiley, 1951. Brogden's procedure follows one originally employed by V.M. Bechterev. See *La Psychologie Objective*, Paris: Alcan, 1913.

16. For some early actual figures see E.R. Hilgard & D.G. Marquis, *Conditioning and Learning*, New York: Appleton-Century-Crofts, 1940.

17. H.D. Kimmel, 'Instrumental factors in classical conditioning', In W.F. Prokasy (ed.), *Classical Conditioning: A Symposium*, New York: Appleton-Century-Crofts, 1965.

18. L.J. Kamin, 'Temporal and intensity characteristics of the conditioned

stimulus', in W.F. Prokasy (ed.) *Classical Conditioning*.

19. W.K. Estes & B.F. Skinner, 'Some quantitative properties of anxiety', *Journal of Experimental Psychology*, 1941, **29**, 390-400. See H. Davis, 'Conditioned suppression: a survey of the literature', *Psychonomic Monograph Supplements*, 1968, **2**, 283-91, for a review of early studies of 'conditioned anxiety'.

20. This technique is now the most popular one in North American investigations of respondent conditioning and provides most of the data for quantitative theories of conditioning. See R.A. Rescorla & A. R. Wagner, 'A theory of Pavlovian conditioning: variations in the effectiveness of reinforcement and non-reinforcement', in A.H. Black & W.F. Prokasy (eds.), *Classical Conditioning II: Current Research and Theory*, New York: Appleton-Century-Crofts, 1972.

21. For specific forms of breakdown of the Law of Intensity, see D.M. Bowden's editorial introduction to V.G. Startsev, *Primate Models of Human Neurogenic Disorders*, Hillsdale, N.J.: Erlbaum, 1976; J.D. Keehn, *Animal Models for Psychiatry*, London: Routledge & Kegan Paul, 1986.

22. D.A. Grant, 'Classical and operant conditioning', In A.W. Melton (ed.), *Categories of Human Learning*.

23. I.P. Pavlov, *Conditioned Reflexes*, 31-2.

24. S.A. Corson *et al.* describe dogs who struggle against Type B conditioning as hyperkinetic, and recommend a course of methamphetamine treatment. See 'Animal models of violence and hyperkinesis', in G. Serban & A. Kling (eds.), *Animal Models in Human Psychobiology*, New York: Plenum, 1976.

25. G. Razran, 'The observable unconscious and the inferable conscious in current Soviet psychophysiology', *Psychological Review*, 1961, **68**, 81-147.

26. E.R. Hilgard & D.G. Marquis, *Conditioning and Learning*, Recent work by R.A. Rescorla reported in the American Psychologist in 1987 suggests that in second-order conditioning CSs are most effective if they relate to each other according to Gestalt laws of perceptual organization.

27. This is a technique for producing conditioned inhibition by a previously neutral stimulus. In the present case, the buzzer inhibits the conditioned excitatory effect of the tactile stimulus.

28. V.S. Merlin, 'The dynamics of "transfer" of conditioned reflex connections from one signal system to the other', in N. O'Connor (ed.), *Recent Soviet Psychology*, London: Liveright, 1961.

29. See N.J. Mackintosh, *Conditioning and Associative Learning*, Oxford: Clarendon Press, 1983, for a review.

30. G. Razran, 'Empirical codifications and specific theoretical implications of compound-stimulus conditioning: perception', in W.F. Prokasy, *Classical Conditioning*.

31. Overshadowing is an important phenomenon for the study of attention. For a review, see N.J. Mackintosh, 'Stimulus control: attention factors', in W.K. Honig & J.E.R. Staddon (eds.), *Handbook of Operant Behavior*, Englewood Cliffs, N.J.: Prentice-Hall, 1977.

32. See H.W. Stevenson, *Children's Learning*, New York: Appleton-Century-Crofts, 1972, for a review of conditioning with children of different ages.

33. I.P. Pavlov, *Conditioned Reflexes*, 51.

34. Detailed studies of investigatory or 'What is it?' reflexes have been described by E.N. Sokolov, *Perception and the Conditioned Reflex*, Oxford: Pergamon Press, 1963.

35. I.P. Pavlov, *Conditioned Reflexes*, 45-7.

36. For a detailed account of Pavlov's typology see M. Macmillan, 'Pavlov's typology', *Journal of Nervous and Mental Disease*, 1963, **137**, 447-54. Regarding Pavlov's vacillations over the typology, see J.A. Gray (ed.), *Pavlov's Typology*.

5. Operant Conditioning: Skinner

1. B.F. Skinner, *The Behavior of Organisms*, New York: Appleton-Century-Crofts, 1938, describes the early work on operant conditioning. Later work is summarized in B.F. Skinner, *Contingencies of Reinforcement*, New York: Appleton-Century-Crofts, 1969. A major change from the early to later work is the shift from purely external stimulus control to the internalization of the external stimulus, particularly in the form of verbal behaviour. See B.F. Skinner, *Verbal Behavior*, New York: Appleton-Century-Crofts, 1957.

2. Two arguments that O *must* be inserted between S and R are that different organisms do not always respond identically to identical stimuli and that the same organism may respond differently to the same stimulus at different times. The arguments are misguided because it is not that O *intervenes* between S and R but that stimuli and responses operate *in the context* of an organism. That context is the history of *that* organism. It is a dynamic context that is unique for each organism.

3. The majority of research studies employing Skinner's concepts and methods are published in the *Journal of the Experimental Analysis of Behavior*. Disputes concerning the replicability of data are rare in this journal. Beginning in 1968, a number of studies on interactions between operant and respondent conditioning have also appeared in this journal. See P.L. Brown & H.M. Jenkins, 'Auto-shaping of the pigeon's key-peck', *Journal of the Experimental Analysis of Behavior* **11**, 1-8. This phenomenon suggests that a Pavlovian CS functions as a substitute for the UCS instead of, or in addition to, predicting its imminence. Autoshaping was subsequently renamed sign-tracking. See E. Hearst & H.M. Jenkins, *Sign-tracking: The Stimulus-Reinforcer Relation and Directed Behavior*, Austin: Psychonomic Society, 1974.

4. A likely candidate to replace the cumulative record in the light of modern chaos theory is the phase portrait, or state space. See M.S. Hoyert, 'Order and chaos in fixed-interval schedules', *Journal of the Experimental Analysis of Behavior*, 1992, **57**, 339-63.

5. From Guy de Maupassant, *The Complete Short Stories*, Garden City, NY: Doubleday, 1955.

6. B.F. Skinner, *The Behavior of Organisms*, 339.

7. W. Kohler, *The Mentality of Apes*, London: Routledge & Kegan Paul, 1925.

8. Under some circumstances it is possible to maintain behaviour that generates electric shocks. See J.W. McKearney, 'Schedule-dependent effects: effects of drugs, and maintenance of responding with response-produced electric shocks', in R.M. Gilbert & J.D. Keehn (eds.), *Schedule Effects: Drugs, Drinking and Aggression*, Toronto: University of Toronto Press, 1972.

9. David Premack has offered an account of reinforcement in terms of the relative probabilities of two responses in a choice situation. In this case, a reinforcer in one situation may not be so in another. See D. Premack, 'Reinforcement theory', in D. Levine (ed.) *Nebraska Symposium on Motivation*, Lincoln: University of Nebraska Press, 1965.

10. An alternative account of conditioned reinforcement is given by R.H. Schuster,

'A functional analysis of conditioned reinforcement', in D.P. Hendry (ed.), *Conditioned Reinforcement*, Homewood, Ill.: Dorsey, 1969.

11. See D.W. Zimmerman, 'Durable secondary reinforcement: method and theory', *Psychological Review*, 1957, **64**, 373-83, for the potency of conditioned reinforcers in response chains where reinforcement is intermittent in each component of the chain.

12. This is the title of a book that introduces, along with others, the schedules herein described. The book contains numerous cumulative records of behaviour (usually pecking by a pigeon) established and maintained by the schedules. See C.B. Ferster & B.F. Skinner, *Schedules of Reinforcement*, New York: Appleton-Century-Crofts, 1957.

13. J.D. Findley & J.V. Brady, 'Facilitation of large ratio performance by use of conditioned reinforcement', *Journal of the Experimental Analysis of Behavior*, 1965, **8**, 125-9.

14. See H.M. Jenkins, 'Sequential organization in schedules of reinforcement', in W.N. Schoenfeld (ed.), *The Theory of Reinforcement Schedules*, New York: Appleton, 1970, pp. 63-109. See also J.E.R. Staddon, 'Temporal control and the theory of reinforcement schedules', in R.M. Gilbert & J.R. Millenson (eds.), *Reinforcement: Behavioral Analyses*, New York: 1972, 209-62.

15. Such schedules would not necessarily provide reinforcement on the occasion of a response but more often in its presence than in its absence. Examples of such schedules can be found in R.J. Herrnstein & P.N. Hineline, 'Negative reinforcement as shock frequency reduction', *Journal of the Experimental Analysis of Behavior*, 1966, **9**, 421-30, and J.D. Keehn & G.E. Coulson, 'Schedule control of alcohol versus water selection by rats', *Quarterly Journal of Studies on Alcohol*, 1972, **33**, 395-9, with negative and positive reinforcement respectively.

16. A novel approach to schedule theory is an account of behaviour reinforced under fixed-interval schedules in terms of chaos theory in physics. M.S. Hoyart, 'Order and chaos in fixed interval schedules of reinforcement', *Journal of the Experimental Analysis of Behavior*, 1992, **57**, 339-63.

17. B.F. Skinner, *Verbal Behavior*, New York: Appleton-Century-Crofts, 1957. Two reviews of this book by K.W. MacCorquodale have been issued as Monograph Supplements to the *Journal of the Experimental Analysis of Behavior*. They are: 'I. B.F. Skinner's *Verbal Behavior*: a retrospective appreciation' (1969) and 'II. On Chomsky's review of Skinner's *Verbal Behavior*' (1970).

18. See J.S. Bruner, *Beyond the Information Given: Studies in the Psychology of Knowing*, New York: Norton, 1973.

19. For a detailed discussion of contingency-shaped and rule-governed behaviour, see 'An operant analysis of problem solving', in B.F. Skinner, *Contingencies of Reinforcement: A Theoretical Analysis*, New York: Appleton-Century-Crofts, 1969.

20. For an operant analysis of verbal behaviour in psychotherapy, see C.B. Ferster, 'Psychotherapy from the standpoint of a behaviorist', in J.D. Keehn (ed.), *Psychopathology in Animals: Research and Clinical Implications*, New York: Academic Press, 1979.

6. The Unconscious after Freud

1. H.J. Eysenck maps the demise of psychoanalysis as a scientific enterprise in *Decline and Fall of the Freudian Empire*, New York: Viking, 1985. As a cultural enterprise it lives in surrealistic art and literature, even if it is not always respected, see J. Berman, *The Talking Cure: Literary Representations of Psychoanalysis*, New York: New York University Press, 1985.

2. C.A. Mace. 'Behaviourism', in A.V. Judges (ed.), *Education and the Philosophic Mind*, London: Harrap, 1957.

3. C. Burt, 'The concept of consciousness', *British Journal of Psychology*, 1962, **53**, 329-42.

4. J.B. Watson, *Behavior. An Introduction to Comparative Psychology*, New York: Holt, 1914. For Watson on the unconscious, see 'The unconscious of the behaviorist', in C.M. Child *et al*, *The Unconscious: A Symposium*, New York: Knopf, 1928.

5. The history is described by J.D. Findley and J.V. Brady, 'Facilitation of large ratio performance by use of conditioned reinforcement', *Journal of the Experimental Analysis of Behavior*, 1965, **8**, 125-9.

6. In contrast to Eysenck and Rachman, Wachtel believes that ' 'The view that behavioural methods are completely alien to the spirit of the psychotherapeutic enterprise is based ... on both an exaggeration of the midwife aspect of the traditional therapist and the surgeon-like qualities of the behavior therapist': P.L. Wachtel, *Psychoanalysis and Behavior Therapy: Towards an Integration*, New York: Basic Books, 1977, 269.

7. These terms were introduced as the compenents of behavioural engineering by L.E. Homme, P.C. Baca, L. Cottingham, & A. Homme, 'What behavioral engineering is', *Psychological Record*, 1968, **18**, 425-34.

8. This translation is from Dudley Fitts, *Aristophanes: Four Comedies*, New York: Harcourt, Brace & World, 1962.

9. An early version of a modern token econony based on contingency management was the so-called *Mark System* proposed by Captain Maconochie for an Australian convict colony in 1846. See his *Crime and Punishment. The Mark System, Framed to Mix Persuasion with Punishment, and Make their Effect Improving, yet their Operation Severe*, London: J. Hatchard & Son, 1846. The basis of the system was that the length of a prisoner's sentence should not be fixed by time but by the marks acquired by his labour.

10. It is ironic that while Freud the writer wanted to be a scientist, Skinner the scientist wanted to be a writer. Skinner wrote a novel, *Walden Two*, and taught a course on the Psychology of Literature early in his career. See D.W. Bjork, *B.F. Skinner: A Life*, New York: Basic Books, 1993, 121.

7. Requiem: And Therefore Never Send to Know

1. C.A. Mace, 'Behaviourism', in A.V. Judges (ed.) *Education and the Philosophic Mind*, London: Harrap, 1957; H.J. Eysenck, *Decline and Fall of the Freudian Empire*, New York: Viking, 1985. Another obituary for behaviourism is B.D. Mackenzie, *Behaviourism and the Limits of Scientific Method*, Atlantic Highlands, N.J.: Humanities Press, 1977. For an analytical review of this book, see G.E. Zuriff, 'The demise of behaviorism – exaggerated rumor?: a review of Mackenzie's *Behaviourism and the Limits of Scientific Method*', *Journal of the Experimental Analysis of Behavior*, 1979, **32**, 129-36. Likewise, a spirited defence of Freud against some of the sources utilized by Eysenck is given by Paul Robinson, *Freud and his Critics*, Berkeley: University of California Press, 1993.

2. D.P. Spence, *The Freudian Metaphor*, New York: Norton, 1987. The quoted

passage begins at the bottom of p. 4. For a positive appraisal of Freud's use of metaphor see David E. Leary, 'Psyche's Muse: the role of metaphor in the history of psychology', in David E. Leary (ed.), *Metaphors in the History of Psychology*, Cambridge: Cambridge University Press, 1990. Laurence D. Smith, 'Metaphors of knowledge and behavior in the behaviorist tradition', describes Skinner's use of metaphor in Chapter 7 of this book and in Chapter 4, Paul McReynolds makes a useful distinction between descriptive, persuasive and creative metaphors. See 'Motives and metaphors: a study in scientific creativity', for a detailed account of uses and abuses of metaphor in science.

3. For a detailed account of Hippocratic and Platonic traditions in medicine, see K. Menninger, M. Mayman, & P. Pruyser, *The Vital Balance*, New York: Viking, 1963.

4. Both Robinson and Eysenck (see n. 1) address this case. A case for hermeneutics and radical behaviourism is suggested by H.L. Miller, Jr., 'Taking hermeneutics to science: prospects and tactics suggested by the work of B.F. Skinner', *Behavior Analyst*, 1994, **17**, 35-42.

5. According to E.G. Boring, *The Physical Dimensions of Consciousness*. New York: Century, 1933, Watson may have shot himself in the foot. On p. 223, Boring says, 'Absurdly paradoxical as it may seem, the context theory of meaning, fathered by Titchener, makes behaviorism, which Titchener excommunicated, the true cognitive psychology.' This may come as a shock to contemporary cognitive psychologists unfamiliar with Skinner's *Verbal Behavior*.

6. H.J. Eysenck & S. Rachman, *The Causes and Cures of Neurosis*, San Diego: Knapp, 1965, 14.

7. B.F. Skinner, 'Why I am not a cognitive psychologist', *Behaviorism*, 1977, **5**, 1-10. J.R. Searle, in *The Rediscovery of the Mind*, Cambridge: Massachusetts Institute of Technology Press, 1992, has another reason for not joining the cognitive psychologists against the behaviourists: 'When they opened up the big black box, they found only a lot of little black boxes inside.' Had he managed to overlook Searle's mistaking the root for the bloom of behaviourism, Skinner might have adumbrated his reasons for not being a cognitive psychologist by reference to ch. 9 of Searle's book. For more militant denunciations of cognitive psychology, see A. Still & A. Costell (eds.), *Against Cognitivism: Alternative Foundations for Cognitive Psychology*, London: Wheatsheaf Harvester, 1991.

8. The earliest explicit interbehavioural psychology was that of Jacob Kantor. For an extensive survey of this system see J.R. Kantor and N.W. Smith, *The Science of Psychology: An Interbehavioral Survey*, Chicago: Principia Press, 1975. A point by point comparison between Kantor's and Skinner's systems is given by E.K. Morris, 'Some relationships between interbehavioural psychology and radical behaviorism', *Behaviorism*, 1982, **10**, 187-216.

9. For a compelling account of the silo metaphor of memory and its dangers see Elizabeth F. Loftus, 'The reality of repressed memories', *American Psychologist*, 1993, **48**, 518-37. Loftus does not discard the memory metaphor but concludes her critique of the validity of repressed memories with the historical observation that the practice of burning witches did not die out until belief in Satan (another metaphor) was discarded. That is, it was not empirical evidence that ended the 'witchcraft craze' but a change of paradigm.

10 In the epilogue to J.D. Keehn (ed.), *Walden 3 or The Prisoners of Venture*, Downsview, Ontario: Masterpress, 1984.

11. Graham Swift, *Ever After*, London, Picador, 1992, 6.

12. See S. Gilman, H. King, R. Porter, G. Rousseau, & E. Showalter, *Hysteria Beyond Freud*, Berkeley, University of California Press, 1993.

13. For further support for this assertion see Mecca Chiesa, *Radical Behaviorism: The Philosophy and the Science*, Boston: Authors Cooperative, 1994, and John Staddon, *Behaviorism: Mind, Mechanism and Society*, London: Duckworth, 1993. Chiesa concentrates on the strengths of Skinner's system, Staddon on its weaknesses. Skinner began with the discovery of order in much of the behaviour of individual organisms; now is beginning the study of behavioural variation that early Skinnerians ignored. See also M.S. Hoyert, 'Order and chaos in fixed-interval schedules of reinforcement', *Journal of the Experimental Analysis of Behavior*, 1992, **57**, 339-63.

Index

Relatedness, existentialism
levels of, 72-3
spatial mode, 69-72
temporal mode, 68
Repetition compulsion, ego defence,
31-2
Repression, ego defence, 18-19, 24-5, 31
Respondent conditioning, 115-40
compound conditioned stimuli, 136-8
conditioned stimuli, 133-4
foundations of, 120-7
operant conditioning compared,
141, 142
response strength, 129-31
temperament, 123, 138-40
unconditioned responses, 128-9
unconditioned stimulus, 131-2
verbal stimuli, 135-6
Watsonian behaviourism and, 5-6
Rogers, C., psychotherapy, 72

Satisfaction, pursuit of, 92-3, 96
Schooling
individual psychology, 84
interpersonal psychiatry, 108-9
Security operations, development of
Self and, 92-6, 106
Sensationism, 3
Sensing function, 48-9, 50, 51
Sexual development *see* Psychosexual
development
Shaw, G.B., conditioning, 116-18
Skakespeare, W., stimulus control,
172-3
Skinner, B.F.
on associations/correlations, 179
Law of Effect, 6, 7
operant conditioning, 141-66, 180;
individual psychology compared,
86-7; interpersonal psychiatry
compared, 88-9, 90, 95, 99, 102;
mands and tacts, 157-8, 159-60,
161-2; rules, 21, 165-6; verbal
behaviour, 95, 102, 154-66, 167
philosophy and, 175-6
Spatial modes, daseinsanalysis, 69-72
Spearman, C.S.
eduction, 100
factor analysis, 54, 55
Spence, D., Freudian metaphor, 177-8

Stebbing, S., philosophy and physics,
175
Structuralism, 3
Sublimation
ego defence, 25-6
interpersonal psychiatry, 107
Sullivan, H.S., interpersonal
psychiatry, 6, 76, 88-112, 180
adolescence, 92, 110-12
childhood, 92, 105-8
children's experiencing modes,
98-100
defining personality, 89-92
development of Self, 92-6
dynamisms, zonal and general
needs, 96-8, 103-5
infancy, 92, 93-6, 98-9, 101-5
juvenile phase, 92, 108-9
preadolescence, 109-10
Superego *see* Ego, superego and id
Symbolism
Adlerian therapy and, 87
ego defence, 28

Tacts, operant conditioning, 102,
157-8, 159, 161
Temperament, conditioning and, 123,
138-40
Temporal dimension
daseinsanalysis, 68-9
psyche in analytical psychology, 50,
52-3
Thinking function, 48, 50, 51
Thorndike, E.L., Law of Effect, 6, 142
Toilet training, 36-7, 94, 105
Transactional analysis, 6-7
Transference, 15-17, 31
daseinsanalysis, 71
parataxic distortions, 100

Undoing, ego defence, 27

Van den Berg, J., 27, 68, 70
Verbal behaviour
analytical psychology, 52-3
free association, 23, 169-70
interpersonal psychiatry, 90,
99-100, 102, 105-6
operant conditioning, 95, 102,
154-66, 167

Index